Stratford Caldecott is founder and
director of the Centre for Faith & Culture at
Westminster College, Oxford. He is assistant
editor of *The Chesterton Review*, and writes
regularly for a number of other Catholic
magazines and journals, including *Communio*,
Catholic World Report and *Inside the Vatican*.

BEYOND THE PROSAIC

BEYOND THE PROSAIC

Renewing the Liturgical Movement

Edited by
STRATFORD CALDECOTT

A PUBLICATION OF
THE CENTRE FOR FAITH & CULTURE
WESTMINSTER COLLEGE, OXFORD

T&T CLARK
EDINBURGH

T&T CLARK LTD
59 GEORGE STREET
EDINBURGH EH2 2LQ
SCOTLAND

First published 1998

ISBN 0 567 08613 5 (HB)
ISBN 0 567 08636 4 (PB)

British Library Cataloguing-in-Publication Data
A catalogue record for this book is available from the British Library

Typeset by Waverley Typesetters, Galashiels
Printed and bound in Great Britain by Bookcraft, Avon

Contents

Introduction

CHRISTOPHER ZEALLEY

Recent liturgical directives from Rome have made concessions to Western-rite Catholics of both progressive and traditional outlook. To take two examples: in 1988 the *motu proprio Ecclesia Dei* gave the green light to a revival of the old Roman rite, and in 1995 official permission was given for the use of altar girls. This trend towards satisfying the demands of Catholics at the two liturgical poles has dismayed Catholics occupying the middle ground: those on the whole satisfied with the *novus ordo,* so long as it is celebrated in a reasonably conservative way.

Normally content to regard the external form of the liturgy as a relatively peripheral concern, such Catholics have for long managed to come to terms, albeit often reluctantly, with successive changes to the *novus ordo,* even when these changes have involved radical breaks with the past. But now a limit to patience seems to have been reached. The permission given for altar girls seems to have brought home to many the power of progressive pressure groups to influence the direction of liturgical development, and dramatically lowered their confidence that Rome will protect the *novus ordo* from further radical change. In these circumstances many conservative Catholics have concluded that support for their viewpoint should be mobilised, and have founded new organisations to achieve this. The strategy adopted by these groupings is not so much to band Catholics together to resist further innovation, as to prepare the intellectual and organisational ground for a revision of the *novus ordo* in a traditional direction.

1

The conference organised in June 1996 by the Centre for Faith & Culture at Westminster College, Oxford, gave a platform to lay people and clerics who are members of, or sympathetic to, these new groupings. Because of the high academic or ecclesiastical standing of many of the participants, and also because the conference on its last day issued an 'Oxford Declaration on the Liturgy' summing up its message, the conference attracted considerable attention from the Catholic press. Moreover, it also bore fruit in the formation of a continuing 'Liturgy Forum' at the Centre for Faith & Culture which will seek to keep the spirit and message of the conference alive in public discussion of liturgical issues.

At the broadest level, as its title, 'Beyond the Prosaic', suggests, the conference's aim was simply to articulate the widespread unease in the Church, at least in the Anglo-Saxon world, with the current state of the vernacular Mass, an unease which intensifies with each new report of decline in church attendance, particularly amongst the young. This concern was linked to a perception that a presentation of Catholicism which focuses primarily on the rational grounds and moral requirements of the faith, while allowing the mystical and devotional dimension only a secondary status, can possess only limited appeal, or at least constitutes a failure to draw on all the resources of tradition in the cause of evangelisation.

The proceedings were also conditioned by the knowledge that a new sacramentary is currently being prepared (it is expected to be issued early in the new century): several participants had been consulted about it. This process of revision presents an opportunity for improving the texts and rubrics of the liturgy which (in principle) is not likely to recur for another generation. The Oxford Declaration to some extent represented an attempt to influence those responsible while there is still time, though there was a consensus that the full achievement of the goals set out is only likely in the longer term, meaning several generations.

There was also an awareness that the high priority now being given to union with the Eastern Orthodox churches has liturgical implications, since (as the members of Eastern Catholic churches present made plain) the new liturgy as currently celebrated constitutes a serious obstacle to ecumenical progress. Participants were informed, for instance, that in Greece the Catholic Church forbids Communion in the hand because the practice scandalises Orthodox Christians.

Finally, the Oxford organisers themselves had clearly found inspiration in the kind of liturgy on offer at the recently established Oxford Oratory, where exclusive use of the new rite is combined with a greater than average recourse to Latin, fine vestments, and traditional chant and music.

The two groupings formed in 1995 in the United States to press for liturgical reform in a conservative direction are Adoremus: The Society for the Renewal of the Sacred Liturgy, and the Society for Catholic Liturgy (SCL). If these bodies had not already begun the process of analysing the current liturgical malaise and searching for solutions, it is unlikely the conference would have happened, and so some introduction to each is important.

Adoremus is supported by such well-known Catholic figures as Fr Joseph Fessio, SJ, of Ignatius Press, Fr Kenneth Baker, editor of *Homiletic and Pastoral Review*, Helen Hull Hitchcock, Ralph McInerny, James Hitchcock and Mother Angelica. It claims theological inspiration from the liturgical writings of Brian Harrison, the author of *Religious Liberty and Contraception* (1988); Mgr Klaus Gamber, whose *The Reform of the Roman Liturgy* (English edition 1993) has reopened serious debate about the basis and desirability of some recent major liturgical changes; and Cardinal Ratzinger, whose foreword to the French edition of Mgr Gamber's book lamented the replacement of organic by 'fabricated' liturgy after the Council. Judging from early newsletters Adoremus is intended to be a popular movement, seeking support from all Catholics concerned about the state of the liturgy.

The Society for Catholic Liturgy was represented at the conference by two of its most eminent supporters: Mgr M. Francis Mannion (its President), a theologian closely associated with Avery Dulles, SJ, and Eamon Duffy, the Cambridge historian whose recent book *The Stripping of the Altars* has established itself as a classic study of liturgical iconoclasm in Reformation England. The SCL has, so far, enjoyed a lower profile than

4

CHRISTOPHER ZEALLEY

Adoremus – perhaps intentionally, given its more academic orientation. Membership is limited to English-speaking 'persons who possess a solid record of scholarship or practical expertise in the area of liturgy or its adjunct disciplines'.

As regards aims and proposals it is clear that the founders of Adoremus are prepared to think much more radically than those of the SCL. Adoremus, to judge from a letter issued by Fr Fessio to invite support (Feast of SS Peter and Paul, 1995), expresses no particular loyalty to the *novus ordo* and aims to 'help the bishops and the Holy See move toward the renewal that should have been'. This will involve 'A complete rethinking and *authentic renewal* of the reform of the liturgy, using both *Sacrosanctum Concilium* and an evaluation of the experience of the post-conciliar years'. Though many liturgical changes since the Council have been pastorally beneficial, 'too many changes have actually distorted the Church's liturgical tradition'. 'Mere insistence on more careful observance of the changes approved since the Council' is explicitly stated *not* to be a sufficient solution to the current problem. Adoremus's immediate aims will be to promote greater understanding of the nature and ceremonies of the Mass through its own publications, and (as an interim measure) to encourage the faithful and beautiful celebration of the current *novus ordo*.

In contrast the SCL in its seventeen-point 'General Philosophy' commits itself to 'the approved revised rites as the basis for any further development', asserts that the 'most pressing' current need in the Church's liturgical life is for 'a more edifying, well-informed and spiritually substantive celebration of the full spectrum of the existing rites', and seeks to foster a renewal of a Catholic ethos in liturgy 'especially in the areas of music, art and architecture'. It hopes to achieve its aims by means of academic study and 'the provision of advice and input to ecclesiastical leadership'.

The conclusions of the Centre's Liturgy Forum were formulated on the last day of the conference and set out in the Oxford Declaration. From this founding charter it is clear that the Liturgy Forum has aligned itself with the radical challenge to the liturgical establishment made by Adoremus and (to a lesser extent) the SCL.

In the first place, it has adopted the view that the *novus ordo* should not necessarily be seen as fulfilling the intentions either of the pre-conciliar liturgical movement or of *Sacrosanctum Concilium*. Rather, the Declaration proclaims that 'in large part' the aims of both have been 'frustrated by powerful contrary forces, which could be described as bureaucratic, philistine and secularist', and that 'the impoverishment of our liturgy after the Council is a fact'. The Declaration makes a further radical commitment by rejecting the recent pattern of liturgical change based on academic, 'drawing-board' reform, and expressing instead the hope that any future reform will be based on an understanding of the *organic* development of the Western liturgical tradition. The sixth article of the Declaration refers to *Sacrosanctum Concilium* 23, which includes the caution: 'care must be taken that any new forms adopted should in some way grow organically from forms already existing'. This emphasis is also found in the SCL's 'General Philosophy', which refers to 'the necessity that liturgical change be organic', and in Fr Fessio's letter of 29 June 1995, where the critical passage from *Sacrosanctum Concilium* 23 is quoted. The need for revived 'organic' development might well be judged the central demand of the Oxford conference, and so the chief guiding principle determining the Liturgy Forum's outlook.

Exactly what 'organic' means in this context may not yet be clear, but one connotation at least is unavoidable: an organic reform must be one which develops from living forms of Catholic worship. In other words, authentic reform will require not only access to a pool of academic liturgical expertise, but also the identification of one or more starting-points in contemporary liturgical forms with a track record of successfully focusing and harnessing popular devotion. In this respect, of course, the revived liturgical movement, as represented by the Liturgy Forum, operates in a wholly different context from the old, in that its starting-point cannot straightforwardly be identified with the current universal liturgy. The mainstream developing life of the new rite, typically featuring monolithic use of the vernacular, folk music settings, altar girls and expanding roles for lay people, is precisely what the conference was seeking an alternative to.

There seem to be three possible starting-points in contemporary liturgy, though each of them is problematic in various ways. One is to be found in the liturgies of the Eastern Catholic churches which – through historical accident – are to be found operating in the West. The conference was notable for the interest displayed in Eastern-rite practice. But however much can be learnt from these liturgies, it would obviously be undesirable in principle and impossible in practice to seek a more universal use of non-Roman rites, even if only as a means for recovering and fostering a greater sense of the sacred in worship. The indigenous Western tradition is so rich in itself that an Eastern starting-point ought to be unnecessary, and it is hard to see Eastern customs being other than extremely alien to most Catholic worshippers.

A second starting-point for renewed development might be some form of conservative new-rite liturgy, in which the *novus ordo* texts are 'decorated' with a selection of the external glories of the old rite. Given that this kind of liturgy has been practised in some places since the early 1970s, and has found some support amongst lay people, it may have plausible claims to being a living liturgy. The SCL tends in the direction of building on this kind of 'aesthetic' approach, and one can see that it might lend to the celebration of Mass a greater sense of the sacred.

There are many problems with this kind of liturgy, however. One may be its tendency to be socially exclusive: it has a reputation for appealing to middle-class people of cultivated aesthetic tastes, and to elements of the young attracted by the 'Brideshead' externals of Church life. But a genuinely Catholic liturgy must always be popular, at least in the sense that its appeal should transcend the influence of social class. Another problem is the unbreakable connection of conservative liturgy to the mainstream development of the new rite. Because the new rite provides its textual and rubrical core, it is subject to new regulations from Rome in the same way as any other mode of celebration of the *novus ordo*. This in practice means that the survival of its special traditional flavour may depend on resisting some of the developments allowed or requested by Church authority. The tension which results is bound to discomfit many people – both priests and laity – who might at first sight think such liturgy desirable. If Rome is resisted, the liturgy becomes un-Catholic in one sense; if she is not, then it becomes un-Catholic in another. The Pope's welcoming of altar girls has brought this tension very painfully to the surface.

There is a further problem in treating conservative new-rite practice as a sound basis for the recovery of authentic Catholic liturgy, for it could be argued that its two dimensions – the text and rubrics of the new rite on the one hand, and the clothing of external forms on the other – are not integrally related. As the conference papers on Gregorian chant made clear, text and music (and by extension the other externals of worship) once had, and ought again to have, a more than extrinsic relation. In the Western Church, at least up until Trent, text and music evolved together over centuries of liturgical development, within a context of popular devotion. But in conservative new-rite liturgy, text and music are simply placed together, each the end-result of a quite separate, artificial process – an imposed academic selection of texts on the one hand, and on the other an arbitrary compromise between participants' aesthetic tastes.

The third option is to build on the revival in use of the 1962 Missal which has followed *Ecclesia Dei*. What has become known as the Tridentine Mass is indubitably a rite which stands at the endpoint of a line of authentic liturgical development. Its continuing vitality has been demonstrated not only by the burgeoning number of indult Masses since 1988, particularly in France and America, but also by the foundation in 1994 of the International Centre for Liturgical Studies (CIEL), the aim of which is to promote academic study of the 'classic' liturgy of the Church. Unsurprisingly, then, there was unanimity at the conference that *Ecclesia Dei* represented a step forward. The SCL view, as expressed by Mgr Mannion, is that this permission for the Tridentine rite should be temporary, lasting only as long as necessary to provide inspiration for the projected re-Catholicisation of the *novus ordo*. But in contrast Adoremus seems to view *Ecclesia Dei* as marking the permanent restoration of the old Roman rite as a feature of Catholic life, and the Declaration for its part called for tolerance of legitimate ritual diversity.

Nevertheless there are problems with taking advantage of the revival of the Tridentine Mass. There is the risk of appearing to endorse a return to a liturgical structure from which the possibility of development is excluded. Some supporters of the old rite assert that the Church acted providentially in finalising the liturgy after Trent because the end of a united Western Christendom meant that healthy organic development could no longer be expected: the intellectual and cultural milieu had changed too greatly. They believe that the best that the Church can do now is preserve the old liturgy intact, because that liturgy encapsulates all the devotional gains of the period in which development was possible. On this view, of course, the 'new cycle of reflection and reform' advocated by the Liturgy Forum would be unnecessary. Moreover the extent to which the 1962 rite currently constitutes a living liturgy seemed to some conference participants debatable, and it is indeed likely that many contemporary Catholics who have never known the old rite would find it, initially at least, as exotic and alien as Eastern-rite liturgy.

The multifarious problems involved in reviving the liturgical movement by building on any of these three sources of non-progressive but living liturgy – the Eastern rites, conservative new-rite practice and the Tridentine movement – indicate the complexity of the issues involved in formulating a convincing alternative to the mainstream development of the *novus ordo*. Clearly a vigorous and lengthy period of discussion is in prospect, and the stance of the Liturgy Forum is likely for the foreseeable future to remain investigative rather than prescriptive. Indeed, the Oxford Declaration calls for caution rather than haste, and appeals to those who love the Catholic tradition to work together in charity, rising above inevitable differences of taste and opinion to a unity that can only be achieved in prayer. Without that basis in prayer and patience, it cannot be expected that the liturgical movement will prosper.

For a genuine *via media* between the old-rite revival on the one hand and liturgical progressivism on the other to be more than a paper theory, it will have to be very thoroughly grounded in a devotionally sensitive as well as professionally researched appreciation of the riches of the inherited Western liturgical tradition. But if all the necessary conditions obtain, and such a grounding is achieved, then perhaps a worthwhile and lasting reform of the Roman rite – the kind of *organic* outgrowth for which the Council called – might finally be realised.

1

The Catholicity of the Liturgy: Shaping a New Agenda

M. FRANCIS MANNION

On a regular basis over the past two decades, the need for a new liturgical movement in Catholicism has been proposed in various quarters. No new movement of the high profile envisaged as desirable by many currently exists and certainly none of those now operational seems entirely capable of unifying the disparate directions proposed for Catholic liturgy as it moves toward the third millennium. What liturgical movement does exist today seems highly diffuse and appears to fan out in a variety of directions. In this essay, I will suggest that, in fact, there exist at present not one but five identifiable liturgical movements in the English-speaking world, particularly in that part with which I am most familiar: the United States. These take the form of five distinct agendas of liturgical reform, which I propose to treat under the following headings: advancing official reform; restoring the pre-conciliar; reforming the reform; inculturating the reform; and recatholicising the reform. An understanding of the character and ideals of the various agendas is a necessary prelude to discussion about the future shape of Catholic liturgical renewal, which, I shall suggest, will be most adequately served by the agenda of *recatholicising the reform.*[1]

It is necessary to preface this analysis with the appropriate cautions about the dangers of a methodology of agenda differentiation. I learned the fundamental elements of this

methodology from my teacher Avery Dulles, who has used such
an approach in many of his writings to bring at least tentative
clarity to complicated theological data.[2] Following Dulles, I
would protest that my aim is neither to suggest clearer lines of
distinction between the various agendas than exist in reality nor
to box individuals and groups in, as though ecclesial life is free
of overlap, complexity and ambiguity. My approach will, I hope,
have the general strengths of the methodology employed,
principally clarity; but it will also have the weaknesses, mainly
simplicity tending toward excessive simplification. I am aware
that the various existing liturgical agendas are not entirely
separate, free of overlap or mutually exclusive. While there
exists a considerable variety of opinions and commitments
within the perspectives I shall identify, it can readily be admitted
that some elements of difference are more a matter of emphasis
or of priority than of fundamental principle. At the same time,
the differences between the various agendas should not be
underestimated. As will become clear, each of these agendas
stands in a particular relationship to the Constitution on the
Sacred Liturgy of the Second Vatican Council, and each may be
seen as based on a particular reading of the Constitution.

The Official Agenda

The first of the agendas currently operative I propose to call
'advancing official reform'. This agenda, which has its roots in
the more theologically- and historically-conscious features of
the modern liturgical movement, was formulated immediately
after the Second Vatican Council and institutionalised in the
Consilium for the Implementation of the Constitution on the
Sacred Liturgy established in 1964, in the Congregation for
Divine Worship in 1969 (under which the Consilium was subsumed), and in the subsequent evolution of that congregation.
Because of its official character, this agenda regards itself with
considerable justification as the legitimate executor of the
programme for liturgical reform set forth in the Constitution
on the Sacred Liturgy. The principal fruits of the official agenda
are the actual revised liturgical books of the Catholic Church as
we now know and celebrate them.

The agenda of advancing official reform is carried out in the work of the Bishops' Committee on the Liturgy in the United States and in the various liturgy secretariats of the English-speaking episcopal conferences.[3] Today this agenda finds notable focus in the deliberations and activities of the International Commission on English in the Liturgy (ICEL), founded during the Council to provide a co-operative agency in translation matters for the episcopates of the English-speaking world.

This agenda operates in liturgical faculties of the more conservative kind, most notable among which is Sant' Anselmo in Rome. Its principal organs include *Ecclesia Orans*, *Notitiae*, the various progress reports and communications from ICEL, and the official newsletters and publications of the liturgy secretariats of the various episcopal conferences. Organisations in the United States such as the Federation of Diocesan Liturgical Commissions and We Believe! are strongly supportive of, and even occasionally defensive about, the official agenda. If the organisations just mentioned belong on the more progressive end of this agenda, it seems fair to say that the present Congregation for Divine Worship and the Discipline of the Sacraments stands on the more conservative end.[4]

The most comprehensive narrative account of the agenda of advancing official reform based on the trajectory established by the post-conciliar Consilium is found in Archbishop Annibale Bugnini's work, *The Reform of the Liturgy 1948–1975*, published in 1990.[5] Indeed, Bugnini himself may be regarded as among the principal authors and advocates of this agenda. His book is probably the most insightful guide to the history of liturgical reform from the Constitution on the Sacred Liturgy through the massive revision of the liturgical books to its present focal point, as far as the English-speaking world is concerned, in the work of ICEL.

The agenda I am describing here is, by its official character, the norm around which the various other agendas I will identify are organised. For this reason, the other agendas may be seen in one way or another as centring on points of criticism or some form of questioning or probing of the official agenda.

In a certain sense, the official agenda is the most challenging to define, because it is so monumental and all-embracing. This agenda operated after the Council, as the Constitution on the Sacred Liturgy indicated it must, with a high and unified theological consciousness in which the liturgical life of the Church was connected more adequately to Trinitarian doctrine, Christology, ecclesiology and eschatology. It followed a path conceived within a set of dialectics: tradition and progress; unity and diversity; simplicity and complexity. An overriding concern was the renewal of the active participation of the Christian people and the need to re-establish diverse ministerial roles within the worshipping assembly. The operational principles of this agenda included arriving at lucidity of liturgical under-standing; recovery of the instructive facility of the liturgy; achieving 'noble simplicity', clarity and brevity; and facilitating freedom from useless repetition and the necessity of much explanation.[6] The inspiration and ideal of the official agenda was the early Roman liturgy, the general features of which it sought to uncover and reappropriate in a methodologically scientific and historically critical manner. The scholarship of this agenda was from the beginning highly ecumenical, drawing upon Orthodox, Anglican and Reformed sources.

Among the more notable features of this agenda since the Council has been its internally evolutionary character. The Consilium in charge of the specific reforms of the various liturgical books regarded its work as both an elaboration and development of the conciliar Constitution on the Sacred Liturgy.[7] The process of evolution found particular expression in the area of language. The conciliar Constitution allowed a very restricted use of the vernacular in the Mass, but it left the way open for appeals to the Holy See by episcopal conferences for more substantive concessions. Accordingly, restrictions on the use of the vernacular were progressively lifted in the face of requests from hierarchies throughout the world, until by 1971 the use of the vernacular in public Masses was left entirely to the judgement of particular conferences.[8]

The present projects of ICEL highlight a second notable feature of the official agenda: the two-phase understanding of the programme of reform that has been operative for nearly two decades. In 1981, ICEL began a process of looking toward the systematic revision of the nearly thirty liturgical books issued since the Second Vatican Council. The current work of ICEL in proposing a new wave of changes is seen by its sponsors as a further legitimate development of the official conciliar and post-conciliar programmes. A key protocol for this aspect of the post-conciliar agenda is found in the opening paragraph of the now controversial 1969 Instruction on the Translation of Liturgical Texts (*Comme le prévoit*), which states that 'after sufficient experiment and passage of time, all translations will need review'.[9] This review process, now well advanced in the English-speaking world, envisages not only new translations but also original texts and some degree of revision of ritual.[10]

Ongoing developments within the official agenda are not, of course, limited to ICEL, or to the English-speaking world. The various initiatives undertaken by the Congregation for Divine Worship and the Discipline of the Sacraments and by other Roman dicasteries, as well as by the Pope himself, are of primary importance. Chief among such developments is the third edition of the Roman Missal currently under preparation.[11] Proposals from a wide variety of scholarly and pastoral sources for additional liturgical reform within the trajectory of the official agenda established after the Second Vatican Council continue to be espoused in conferences and publications.[12]

We turn now to the two agenda groups that exist on the conservative or traditionalist end of the spectrum of present-day liturgical movements. The first of these is committed to what I shall call 'restoring the pre-conciliar'.

Traditionalism and Restoration

Among the restorationist agenda groups, there exists a fundamental suspicion of the Second Vatican Council and of the Constitution on the Sacred Liturgy, and therefore of all liturgical developments, both theoretical and practical, subsequent to 1963. To greater or lesser degree, a conviction operates among adherents of this agenda group that the authentic liturgy of Catholicism has been compromised since the Second Vatican Council and that the Mass of 1969 is fundamentally objectionable because it is neither in continuity with the pre-conciliar liturgical order nor an adequate expression of the fullness of the mystery of faith.[13]

The followers of Archbishop Marcel Lefebvre and the clerical Society of St Pius X, which include a diverse following in the English-speaking world, represent the more extreme exponents of the restorationist agenda. These are unambiguously and unalterably committed to the return of the so-called Tridentine Mass; no other avenue of liturgical development is acceptable.[14] This wing of the restorationist agenda fundamentally rejects the ability of any Pope to reform the Tridentine Mass and, for that reason, it objects in principle to the Missal of Paul VI.[15] Apologists of this school have argued variously that the Mass of Paul VI must be rejected due to its Protestant inspiration, its formal invalidity and the defective priestly intention it enshrines. The new Mass is said to be a symbol of resurgent modernism and an instrument of revolutionary errors in the Church.[16]

Not all who espouse the restoration of the pre-conciliar have been so radical in their objections to liturgical reform.[17] Many Catholics whose loyalty to the Holy See remained strong forthrightly sought the restoration of the Tridentine Mass after 1970 without rejecting out of hand the Missal of Paul VI. All in all, however, Catholics of this persuasion remain most suspicious of the Second Vatican Council and are deeply disappointed in what the post-conciliar liturgical reforms have produced. The leadership of the Latin Liturgy Association in the United States expressed this outlook pointedly in writing recently that the Constitution on the Sacred Liturgy belongs to a set of 'fallible human documents written by fallible human bishops as a result of a process which was not devoid of politicking'.[18] In the writer's opinion, 'much harm has been done to the Church by regarding the conciliar documents as the Revealed Word of God'.[19] The commentary continued, 'There is clearly no consensus within the Church on the important question of the Council's liturgical reforms',[20] and it concluded: 'The ranks of those who regard the conciliar program on liturgy as being quite ill conceived are not limited to the ignorant and the embittered.'[21]

The 1984 Vatican indult allowing the use of the old Mass under strictly controlled conditions and the more generous 1988 document *Ecclesia Dei* were proposed largely in response to increasing expressions of disaffection and even defection on the part of traditionalist Catholics.[22] The official provisions for the Tridentine Mass since 1984 seem to have provided some relief from the tense situation that was developing in Catholic traditionalist circles. A consequence was the reconciliation with the Holy See of some followers of Archbishop Lefebvre, creating in 1988 the Priestly Fraternity of St Peter, now found in a number of dioceses in the United States and Europe. The traditionalist Benedictine monastery of Ste-Madeleine in Le Barroux in France seems to have become a centre for those following and promoting the pre-conciliar rite.[23] Groups in the United States such as the Coalition in Support of *Ecclesia Dei* and the Traditional Mass Society have proposed initiatives, as yet unsuccessful, to advance a separate vicariate system for Catholics who seek a complete restoration of all features of the liturgical life of the Church existing before the Second Vatican Council.[24]

The activities and perspectives of this agenda group may be gleaned from papers and newsletters such as *The Wanderer, The Remnant, Precious Blood Banner* and *The Latin Mass.* Very little scholarly material has up to now been available in support of liturgical restorationism. The outlook of this agenda group calls to mind what scripture scholar Raymond Brown has described in other circumstances as 'non-scholarly conservatism'.[25] This does not mean that this agenda should therefore be dismissed; it is simply to recognise that it has a popular rather than an academic base. However, a movement to provide a scholarly foundation for this agenda seems to be under way more recently. While the centre of such activities is Europe, notably France and Germany, developments are followed with a lively interest in traditionalist Mass circles in the United States. The movement Renaissance Catholique in France has taken the initiative of organising in Paris, with the support of Cardinals Alfons Stickler and Silvio Oddi, the International Centre for Liturgical Studies (CIEL), which seeks to provide a theological defence of the Tridentine Mass.[26]

William D. Dinges estimates that there are over 375 Tridentine Mass centres in the United States and that these are
attended by between 15,000 and 20,000 Catholics. Nearly half
of these centres are unauthorised, while the rest operate with
official ecclesiastical approval. About half of American dioceses
now sponsor regularly celebrated Tridentine Masses.[27]

Probably the mildest form of the restorationist agenda is that
espoused by an indeterminate body of Catholics who have
learned to live with the Mass of 1969, but whose preference
would be for the Tridentine Mass.[28] Those who espouse the
restoration of the pre-conciliar liturgy do not always argue for
the discontinuation of the Mass of Paul VI; for some the co-
existence of the various orders of the Mass is both acceptable
and desirable.[29]

Reforming a Reform

Not everyone on the conservative or traditionalist end of the
spectrum of liturgical positions is a restorationist. A much more
moderate grouping is committed to what has been described as
'reforming the reform'. This expression was popularised with
the appearance of the book *The Reform of the Roman Liturgy* by
Mgr Klaus Gamber, published in English in 1993.[30]

The reform of the reform does not seek to restore the
Tridentine Mass, but rather to return to what it regards as the
true intentions of the Constitution on the Sacred Liturgy and to
review in depth the processes and actual achievements of the
liturgical reform. The proponents of this agenda have in
common with Tridentine restorationism a strong, if less radical,
dislike of much of what came after the Second Vatican Council,
but, unlike the restorationists, they insist that they embrace
fundamentally the vision of the Council and the Constitution
on the Sacred Liturgy. The critical concerns of this group are
the programmatic decisions and initiatives of the post-conciliar
Consilium and the character of the reformed liturgical books
themselves. The central programme espoused in this agenda
appears to be a revisitation of the 1962 Missal (and its 1965 and
1967 amendments) and a revision of the order of Mass in a less
severe direction than actually occurred, in light of what

proponents perceive to be the true intentions of the pre-conciliar liturgical movement and of the Second Vatican Council.

The broad lines of this agenda are set out as follows by Gamber:

> It is generally accepted that, in one way or another, a liturgical reform, particularly an enrichment of the Roman rite, had become necessary because, since the Council of Trent, it had become ossified into a form of rubricism. There is also a consensus that the Constitution on the Sacred Liturgy of the Second Vatican Council corresponded in many respects to the legitimate pastoral requirements of our time. But no such consensus exists when we look at the reforms that were actually introduced, particularly the new liturgical books composed by a group of experts after the conclusion of the Council.[31]

Gamber's book contains a testimonial by Mgr Wilhelm Nyssen that sharply identifies the focus of Gamber's discontent: '[Gamber] deplored the post-conciliar *Instructions for the Implementation of the Constitution* because he felt that they had been published with undue haste, that their content was shallow, and that much of it was manifestly incompetent.'[32]

The agenda to reform the reform has been taken up in the United States by Father Joseph Fessio and the leaders of the organisation Adoremus: Society for the Renewal of the Sacred Liturgy. Adoremus is, in its own words, committed to 'a complete rethinking and *authentic renewal* of the reform of the liturgy, using both *Sacrosanctum Concilium* and an evaluation of the experience of the post-conciliar years to arrive at a renewed liturgy in keeping with the principles of the Second Vatican Council'.[33] The guiding prescription invoked is Article 23 of the Constitution on the Sacred Liturgy, which states: 'There must be no innovations unless the good of the Church genuinely and certainly requires them, and care must be taken that any new forms adopted should in some way grow organically from forms already existing.'[34] This principle is clearly thought to have been offended against in the agenda of official reform.

As with the other agendas, a spectrum of positions exist within this one and a variety of perspectives are espoused. The actual project of reforming the reform has not by any means achieved complete clarity or unanimity. However, the leaders of this movement appear to share a common conviction that liturgical renewal has gone beyond anything legitimately envisaged by the Second Vatican Council; that the episcopate has in liturgical matters abdicated its authority to specialists and scholars; that ICEL bears much responsibility for the current state of affairs; and that an order of the Mass more closely related to the 1962 Missal than to the Mass of 1969 is desirable.

A more detailed account of how, in regard to the Mass, the reform of the reform might be carried out is found in the first issues of *Adoremus Bulletin*, which featured a three-part essay by Father Brian W. Harrison in late 1995 and early 1996. Harrison espouses the position of Gamber that the Roman rite has been destroyed in the post-conciliar reforms and that a new rite of the Mass should now be created and instituted, 'having *equal status and recognition* with the rite introduced by Paul VI'.[35] This new rite would not displace the Mass of 1969, but would be regarded as 'an alternative implementation of Vatican Council II'.[36] Toward this end, Harrison calls for a modification of the Missal of 1962 in light of the principles of the Constitution on the Sacred Liturgy. Among his proposals are the following: the restoration of the recitation of the Canon in Latin; exclusive use of the Roman Canon; the restriction of communion to one species; priest and people facing in the same direction during the eucharistic liturgy; the use of two Scripture readings instead of three; and the exclusive use of men in liturgical ministries.[37]

I am uncertain how widely shared these proposals are in this agenda group. Overall, my impression is that the directions outlined by Gamber and Harrison are received with considerable sympathy by many who speak generally of 'reforming the reform'. Cardinal Joseph Ratzinger wrote a preface to the French, but not the English, edition of Gamber's book and has spoken positively of Harrison's proposals. Dominican theologian Aidan Nichols has suggested a direction similar to Harrison's in his recent book, *Looking at the Liturgy*, written to advance the proposal to reform the reform.[38] Fessio, who is probably the leader of this agenda in the United States, focuses the reform of the reform on three central measures: priest and people facing in the same direction; the use of the Roman

Canon with a minimum of options; and the re-institution of the sung Gregorian chant Ordinary of the Mass.[39] However, unlike Gamber and Harrison, Fessio and the leadership of Adoremus seem less intent on a return to the 1962 Missal as the point of departure than on seeking a normative re-ordering of the Mass of 1969 along lines inspired by the 1962 Missal and its 1965 and 1967 revisions. This would inevitably involve some structural changes in the present order of liturgy.[40]

I want to turn now to the two agenda groups that represent respectively progressive and corrective programmes for ongoing liturgical reform. The first of these may be described as committed to 'inculturating the reform' and the second to what I propose to call 'recatholicising the reform'. What both of these agenda groups have in common is a fundamental affirmation of the Second Vatican Council and the Constitution on the Sacred Liturgy, as well as an *acceptance of the reformed rites as they now exist as the basis for any further development.* Unlike the two conservative groups – which wish more or less to go back to or behind the Council – the two groups which I am now introducing seek to go beyond the reform as it has been carried through in recent decades, but in rather different ways.

Worship, Culture and Creativity

The fundamental conviction operative in the agenda of 'inculturating the reform' is that while the revisions of the past thirty years have more or less successfully given the Church a new set of liturgical books, these achievements are but a prelude to a much more profound and far-reaching reform of the liturgy. An entirely new phase of creativity must be initiated by which the officially revised liturgical rites will be adapted to the various cultures of the world, including those of the modern West. This position proposes a new pluralisation, diversification and decentralisation of Catholic liturgical life.

I stated at the outset that a certain overlap may be identified in the relationship between the various agendas described in this essay. This is evident in the connection between the official agenda and the inculturation agenda. The latter does not simply take up where the former leaves off. If the roots of the inculturation agenda are in the official reform, it is clear that the official agenda – notably in regard to the translation processes that have engaged ICEL and the English-speaking bishops' conferences – embraces at least in principle the beginnings of liturgical inculturation.[41] Yet it may be argued that the thoroughgoing inculturation ideals as they are now developing in academic circles go considerably beyond the present scope of the official agenda.[42]

The positions espoused within the agenda of inculturation are as diverse as in the other groups. Some envisage the need to adjust the Roman liturgy to modern Western European and North American tastes and conceptions. This concern was central to the meeting in Scottsdale, Arizona in December 1974 that gave rise to the North American Academy of Liturgy.[43] Others focus on the necessity of liturgical adaptation to the religious ethos of particular cultural communities within the United States, for instance, African-American, Hispanic and Native American.[44] Dialogue between feminist theology and spirituality and Catholic liturgical tradition represents a particularly strong movement within the inculturation agenda. The need for 'inclusive' gender language both in relation to God and the human person generally provides the focal point in this area.[45] Likewise, those influenced by liberation and political theologies bring their own set of concerns to the liturgical inculturation agenda.[46]

The spirit of experimentation and adaptation that has characterised liturgical celebration at the parish level in the United States since the Second Vatican Council may be understood as inculturation, even if it is not consciously adverted to as such. Popular styles of priestly presidency, preaching, music and art, as well as the advent of small-group dynamics in the liturgy, represent an absorption into Catholic worship of celebrative idioms native to popular American culture. As the Roman liturgy is adapted to the mainstream culture of the United States, it becomes notably 'informal' and personalised and a high value is placed on stylistic creativity and variety.

The inculturation agenda claims theoretical legitimacy by reference to Articles 37–40 of the Constitution on the Sacred Liturgy, which talk about the need for renewal to proceed beyond a reform of the liturgical books to an adaptation of those books to new cultural circumstances. The intention of the Second Vatican Council, it is argued, was not only to recover the historic core of the Roman rite but also to adapt the liturgy to new and diverse cultural environments. Article 37 of the Constitution states: 'The Church does not wish to impose a rigid uniformity in matters which do not involve the faith or the good of the whole community. Rather does she respect and foster the qualities and talents of the various races and nations.'[47] Accordingly, 'anything in these peoples' way of life which is not indissolubly bound up with superstition and error she studies with sympathy, and, if possible, preserves intact. She sometimes even admits such things into the liturgy itself, providing they harmonise with its true and authentic spirit'.[48]

Once the substantial unity of the Roman liturgy is safeguarded, the Constitution declares, 'provision shall be made, when revising the liturgical books, for legitimate variations and adaptations to different groups, regions and peoples, especially in mission countries'.[49] Article 40 allows for even more radical adaptation of the rites and prescribes that local ecclesiastical authority must 'carefully and prudently consider which elements from the traditions and cultures of individual peoples might appropriately be admitted into divine worship'.[50] The same article indicates that this process should be carried out through a programme of approved experimentation and involve the input of experts in cultural adaptation.

At the international level, Father Anscar Chupungco remains the most notable and respected theoretical proponent of the inculturation agenda.[51] This agenda is widely embraced in the better-known graduate programmes in liturgy in the United States, and it finds strong advocacy in the nation's Catholic Black, Hispanic and Native American organisations, as well as in various research projects and conferences, both academic and pastoral.[52]

Catholicity and the Liturgy

This brings me to the fifth and final agenda, which I describe as 'recatholicising the reform'. At this point, I move from a descriptive to a prescriptive mode. As I stated at the outset, I believe that ongoing liturgical reform will be most adequately advanced by the agenda I am now introducing. As will become clear, the recatholicising agenda draws on elements of the agendas already described, indicating again that the agendas are not necessarily mutually exclusive. In the final section of this essay, in which an evaluation of the various agendas will be offered, I shall argue that among the strengths of the recatholicising agenda is that it unifies with a considerable degree of adequacy the perceived values of the other agendas.

The words 'recatholicising' and 'recatholicisation' invoke the understanding of 'catholicity' found in such theologians as Avery Dulles and Henri de Lubac, for whom the catholicity of the Church is found not primarily in its geographic extensiveness, but in the spiritual depth, sacramental richness, religious exuberance and creativity of ecclesial institutions.[53] Avery Dulles's magisterial work, *The Catholicity of the Church*, published in 1985, provides the immediate inspiration, as far as nomenclature is concerned, for the agenda I am describing here.[54] In this book, Dulles presents a rich and compelling vision of the catholicity of the Church. When the Church is truly catholic, it is characterised by a high Trinitarian consciousness; it reaches into the very depths of the human soul; it engages profoundly the spiritual heritage of historic Christianity; and its vision is centred on the glory of God and the coming of the Kingdom.

Dulles introduces his analysis of ecclesial catholicity as follows: 'As we read in the Letter to the Ephesians, Paul prays that his readers may be enabled to comprehend "the breadth and length and height and depth" of the love of Christ, even though this "surpasses knowledge" (Ephesians 3:18–19). Like the love of Christ, the Church may be viewed as a mystery with four dimensions: height, depth, breadth, and length' (p. 30). First there is 'catholicity from above' or 'the "height" of catholicity'. By 'catholicity from above', Dulles means that 'the triune God, who communicates himself in the incarnate Word and in the Holy Spirit, is the source and ground of catholicity' (p. 47). The catholicity of the Church is constituted in this dimension by the glory of God flowing in its Trinitarian dynamism into the whole earth. Out of the fullness of love, God bounteously and splendidly shares His life with created beings, so that in Him 'we live and move and have our being' (Acts 17:28). In this marvellous and all-encompassing Trinitarian movement, Dulles says, the Word of God 'entered into a kind of union with the cosmos' (p. 34). Christ becomes the 'head of creation' (p. 34) and 'the Church is the fullness or completion of Christ' (p. 41). The Church is then understood as 'a participation in Christ's dynamic power to recapitulate both humanity and the cosmos under his universal headship' (p. 43).

Turning next to the depth dimension of the Church, Dulles introduces 'catholicity from below' in the following manner: 'According to the Catholic understanding, the Spirit of God does not merely hover above the world, nor does it simply touch the world as a tangent touches a circle, but it reaches into the depths. Divine life, when it enters the human realm, penetrates not only the spiritual faculties of intellect and will, but the person's whole being, including the sensory and bodily aspects' (p. 48). Catholicity from below is constituted by the truth that 'justification stands in a cosmic setting' (p. 51). In this regard, Dulles identifies in Catholicism a profound 'reverence for human nature' (p. 53), for the bodily, the sensory and the beautiful. Human nature and the created order have an internally transcendental orientation and are 'intrinsically ordered toward the goal of eternal blessedness in God through Christ' (p. 57; cf. pp. 55ff.). Dulles here attends to what might be described as ecclesial anthropology, 'the human material that goes into the Church' (p. 48).

The quantitative or horizontal aspect of catholicity, what Dulles calls 'catholicity in breadth', is treated next. This dimension refers to the expansive and inclusive features of the Church, to the intrinsic ability of the Church 'to communicate itself without limit to persons of every kind and condition' (p. 68). Dulles points out, quoting de Lubac, that in this sense the Church was as catholic on the day of Pentecost as it was ever to become in the course of history (p. 68). For Dulles, 'The catholicity of the Church became manifest when the Gentiles turned to the gospel as giving the answers to their own questions about the meaning of life and death. Subsequent history has confirmed the capacity of men and women of every kind and

condition to find faith and hope in the Christian proclamation'
(p. 73). Furthermore, 'As the Church spreads her faith, she
shows forth the transcendence of the gospel and the universal
working of the grace of the Holy Spirit. At the same time, the
Church actualises her own catholicity. Constituted in the world
as a sacrament, or efficacious sign, of God's universal redemp-
tive will in Christ, the Church is driven by an inner dynamism to
represent the whole of humanity as the recipient or redemption' (p. 74). There is thus 'in the church a universality in her
capacity as sign' (p. 74).

Dulles turns finally to what he calls 'catholicity in length' or
'catholicity in time' (p. 87). He points to St Thomas Aquinas's
assertion that the Church, on the one hand, has existed since
the time of Abel and, on the other, that it stretches forward into
eternity, into eschatological fulfilment (cf. pp. 87–89). In the
New Testament, the dynamic eschatological vision was symbolised in the language of the marriage of the Lamb, the
heavenly banquet, the Sabbath rest, the New Jerusalem, the
completed Temple (p. 90). Dulles recognises that 'Catholic
theology has not always found it easy to come to terms with the
realities of history' (p. 99). The dangers of an exaltation of
the past at the expense of the present and of the present
over the past are perennial in Christian history (pp. 94ff.). In
its Constitution on Divine Revelation, the Church at the
Second Vatican Council opted for 'a dynamic, progressive
view of tradition', avoiding both of the dangers just mentioned
(p. 100; cf. pp. 101–03). The Church, accordingly, is called to
'show forth in the world the mystery of the Lord in a faithful
though shadowed way, until at last it will be revealed in total
splendor' (Constitution on the Church, p. 8). Dulles calls,
then, for both a positive theological appreciation of Catholic
history and the renewal of a strong eschatological vision (pp.
90–94).

Clearly Dulles's analysis of catholicity is not the only one
that might be invoked profitably, and his concerns are not
immediately liturgical.[55] Yet the kind of comprehensive vision
of ecclesial catholicity that Dulles sets forth provides an appropriate theological grounding for the agenda of recatholicising
the reformed liturgy.

How does this agenda differ from the others? Unlike the conservative or traditional agendas, the recatholicisation of the reform shares with the inculturation agenda the conviction that the reforms of the liturgical books since the Second Vatican Council are fundamentally to be welcomed and embraced, even as they need to be subject to some further development. However, the nature of the direction in which further development ought to proceed is what distinguishes the recatholicisation and inculturation agendas from each other. If the inculturation agenda is committed to a substantive adaptation of the revised rites to diverse cultural situations, the recatholicising agenda is primarily committed to a vital re-creation of the ethos that has traditionally imbued Catholic liturgy at its best – an ethos of beauty, majesty, spiritual profundity and solemnity.[56] In this, the recatholicising framework is not unsympathetic to the inculturation agenda – even if it does regard the actual achievements of that agenda with considerable reserve. In fact, it incorporates the fundamental principles of inculturation set out in the Constitution on the Sacred Liturgy.

The recatholicising agenda is also open to what it regards as the positive prescriptions of the ongoing agenda of official reform, for instance, better translations; yet its primary interest is not with the creation of new texts or translations or with modifications of ritual and expanding options.[57] The recatholicising agenda, unlike the other four, sets no great store on further structural change in Catholic worship at this time – whether in 'conservative' or 'progressive' directions. This agenda seeks, instead, a period of settling down and intensive pastoral appropriation now that the liturgical books have been thoroughly and systematically revised. In this respect, it embraces a highly conservative view of the dynamics of liturgical change, holding that ritual functions best when it is familiar and predictable.[58] Accordingly, proponents of this agenda tend to regard the various present proposals for further revision as potentially disorienting and destabilising of the Church's public worship and as vitiating the 'competence in ritual' of congregations.[59]

What fundamentally distinguishes the recatholicising agenda from the other four is that it regards the principal challenge of ongoing liturgical reform as *spiritual* rather than *structural.* The recatholicisation agenda stands for a spiritual broadening and deepening of the post-conciliar liturgical order set forth in the revised books. It does not regard that order as by any means perfect. It does view it, however, as eminently worthy of reception by the whole Church in the post-conciliar era and as expressive of spiritual riches in great part unappreciated and untapped. This agenda seeks an intensive rather than extensive renewal of the liturgy, by which is meant a spiritual unfolding of the potentiality of the revised liturgical rites rather than their expansion with new texts, ceremonies and symbols.[60]

Recatholicisation means renewing the spiritual, mystical and devotional dimensions of the revised rites. It seeks a recovery of the sacred and the numinous in liturgical expression which will act as a corrective to the sterility and rationalism of much modern liturgical experience.[61] This agenda calls for a new attention to the phenomenology of religion and the sacred, of the kind represented earlier in this century by such figures as Gerardus van der Leeuw, Rudolf Otto and Mircea Eliade, who seem out of fashion among liturgists today.[62] The programmatic elements just described may be subsumed theologically under the category of liturgical pneumatology – a feature of Western liturgy which remains decidedly underdeveloped, despite often-expressed intentions in the modern liturgical movement to correct this deficiency.[63]

The aesthetic dimension of worship represents another area in which the catholic expressivity of the liturgy needs considerable attention. As Eastern thinkers often point out, the Christian West tends to regard the aesthetic as extrinsic to the constitution of the liturgy. Thus a new commitment to liturgical aesthetics – by means of which the aesthetic will move from the status of an accidental to a constitutive element of liturgy – remains today a critical need.[64] Encouraging grounds for such a development are found in the considerable interest being accorded the aesthetic in Western theology today, even if surprisingly little attention is paid to the liturgy in the process.

Once noted for its excessive rubricism, Western liturgy of late has become subject to anti-ritual bias, so that there does not exist today an adequate theology of ceremonial in Catholic liturgical life. This deficiency may be corrected by drawing on aesthetic theory, as well as on those strands of ritual studies sympathetic to Catholic sacramentality.[65] In tandem with the correction of this problem is the necessity of recovering a sense of the sacramental objectivity of the liturgy, so that liturgical rites are not regarded as human fabrications, but as 'God's masterpieces' or the 'masterworks of God'.[66]

This agenda looks to a renewal of the eschatological orientation in Catholic worship wherein the connection between the heavenly and earthly liturgies is again encountered.[67] One of the most remarkable features of the pre-conciliar liturgical movement was the resurgence of interest in the eschatological character of Christian worship, generated in great part by a new appreciation of the liturgical life of the East. Yet that interest seemed to be diverted soon after the Second Vatican Council as eschatology began to be secularised and politicised, and as Catholic life and worship generally began to refocus in the direction of relevance to modern culture.[68]

Related to the eschatological is the renewal of the cosmic sense in the liturgy. Catholic liturgy today notably suffers from a shrunken cosmic consciousness and a shrunken cosmic ritualisation. A more adequate cosmic expressivity will serve to draw all of creation, including the saintly and the angelic, into the framework of worship.[69] A renewed cosmic emphasis will help overcome the present tendency of liturgical celebration toward privatisation and congregationalist self-referentiality and self-enclosure.[70]

Recatholicisation means a renewal of the doxological, praise-filled character of worship capable of rescuing present-day liturgical practice from its excessively pragmatic, didactic and functional conceptions. The fundamental impulses for doxology, I would argue, are found in eschatological and cosmic conceptions. When eschatological and cosmic vision is narrowed or collapses, then the doxological amplitude and expressivity of Christian worship is vitiated. In turn, the lack of doxological vision leads to a failure of Christian imagination and to the radical impoverishment of the whole programmatic fabric of the liturgy.[71]

Practically, the recatholicising agenda means taking the present rites and working to celebrate them in a much more profound, dignified and spiritually edifying manner than has generally been the case since the advent of post-conciliar revision. It requires a deepening of the liturgical competence of congregations;[72] provision for the training of laity to assume more appropriately the ministries provided them in liturgical celebrations; and, not least, improving the standards of priestly leadership and preaching.

A renewed movement to provide for a more noble character in liturgical music and to restore a Catholic ethos to places of worship by creative contact with the longer traditions of Catholic art and architecture is required by the recatholicisation agenda.[73] While the modern movement in art and architecture and ritual-functionalism in music have served to correct some expressive excesses in the past, the time has come to move beyond them and to seek an artistic renaissance of a richer and more imaginative kind than that seen so far in the post-conciliar liturgy.

Not least, the recatholicising agenda implies a new respect for the longer tradition of Catholic liturgical history, including the medieval, baroque and post-Tridentine eras. Taking the catholicity of the Church seriously means overcoming the excessive tendency of modern liturgical scholarship to stake so much on the search for normative historic origins, and the corresponding tendency toward a severe bias against almost everything that came after the patristic era. The conviction still obtains among liturgists that little of positive value is to be learned from Catholic liturgical life for most of the second millennium. However, for a new generation of historians such as Eamon Duffy, these more 'recent' liturgical traditions are less easily dismissed than has been the case for much of the twentieth century.[74]

The recatholicising agenda operates from a conviction that some important features of the pre-conciliar liturgical movement were not adequately appreciated in the period of revision after the Second Vatican Council. Thus it seeks to establish contact with neglected strands of the twentieth-century liturgical movement associated with figures like Romano Guardini, Louis

Bouyer and Virgil Michel and with the authors of the patristic revival.[75]

While present-day inspiration for the recatholicisation agenda comes from diverse sources, the writings of Hans Urs von Balthasar and the theological interests associated with the international *Communio* network are notably important.[76] The liturgical theology, spirituality and aesthetics of the Christian East, both Catholic and Orthodox, can be expected to play a considerable role.[77] As is evident from this brief sketch, this agenda is well served by liturgical scholars from the Anglican and Protestant traditions. Liturgical organisations sympathetic to the recatholicising agenda include the Society for Catholic Liturgy, formed in 1995.

Evaluative Conclusion

At the beginning of this essay, I declared my preference for the agenda of recatholicising the reform. This position does not, however, seek simply to invalidate the other agendas. Indeed, my stated preference is founded on my positive judgement of the ability of the fifth agenda to incorporate the strengths of the other four. My final task here is to suggest strengths and weaknesses in the various agendas and to suggest how the strengths may be unified in the agenda of recatholicising the reform.

What may be said about the agenda of advancing official reform? It can certainly claim strong legitimacy by reference to the Constitution on the Sacred Liturgy and to the post-conciliar decisions of ecclesiastical authority in interpreting the Constitution as the liturgical books were being revised. Like most liturgists and sacramental theologians, I believe this agenda deserves strong support in most of its fundamental features. The liturgical books as revised represent overall a heroic achievement. In my opinion, the movement toward the vernacular, the restoration of the chalice to the people, the opening up of liturgical ministries to the laity and the clarification of the structure of the various sacramental rites were developments of monumental importance. The various principles and achievements of this agenda provide, not least, the fundamental basis for the recatholicising agenda espoused here.

The official agenda may be criticised, however, for the reasons that it seemed to have proceeded somewhat hastily; promoted a too rapid evolution of the programmatic trajectory of Vatican II; was hampered by an excessively negative reading of the pre-conciliar liturgy; and was limited by an inordinately verbal and rationalistic understanding of Christian worship. Methodologies informed by mechanistic and functionalist models of ritual, as well as by didacticism in conceptualisations of liturgical participation, seem to have been operative to a severe degree after the Council.[78] The progress of this agenda is today no less than in past decades marred by a tendency toward bureaucratic management, so that the leadership of national and international liturgical commissions easily takes on the appearance of a 'knowledge class', that is, a class of self-validating technical experts lacking appropriate sensitivity to non-theoretical matters, including popular sentiment on issues of worship.[79] What is not unfairly called 'the liturgical establishment' tends to be somewhat authoritarian in outlook and adversarial toward contrary theoretical and practical perspectives on liturgical reform – even of the more reasonable and well-informed kind. This agenda is increasingly the subject of criticism, which it has not for the most part taken well, even when such criticism comes from the Holy See. The necessary survival of the programme of official reform requires that it proceed more dialogically, self-critically and openly *vis-à-vis* the other agendas than it has done hitherto and that it moderate itself in light of their legitimate aims and ideals.

What of the agenda of restoring the pre-conciliar? I think it most unlikely and, indeed, very undesirable that the restoration of the pre-conciliar liturgy could become a major agenda item for future liturgical developments. A return to the pre-conciliar liturgy would intrinsically involve a rejection of fundamental commitments made by the Second Vatican Council. Liturgical practice is more than a matter of taste or personal spirituality; it embodies a whole set of theological and ecclesiological principles and convictions. For this reason, the present allowance of the Tridentine Mass seems to me legitimate only as a temporary measure. The prescriptions of *Ecclesia Dei* must of necessity give way eventually to the renewing vision of the Second Vatican Council. However, those who seek the celebration of the Missal of 1962 deserve in the meantime more pastoral care, understanding and respect than local ecclesiastical leaders have been hitherto willing to accord. A more sympathetic and dialogical spirit on the part of bishops and pastors would probably have the effect on many traditionalist Catholic groups of softening resistance to post-conciliar changes and of leading them to a more co-operative and receptive outlook on the Second Vatican Council.

Yet, the desire of the restorationist agenda to recover the transcendent character and sacred ethos of the Church's worship and to renew an atmosphere of reverence, awe, majesty and solemnity is to be commended and embraced. Those who advocate a return to the pre-conciliar liturgy rightly criticise the lack of those features in the practice of the reformed rites. The Church's heritage of art, architecture and music, as the Council insisted, must be maintained and developed. The recatholici-sation agenda shares with the restorationist movement strong common concerns in these areas. The restorationist agenda also highlights the fairly widespread abuses in the liturgical practice of the reformed rites. The degree to which some Catholics have resisted the revised rites and taken recourse to the traditionalist movement because of liturgical abuse merits considerable reflection. Ecclesiastical leaders would do well to redouble efforts to re-establish liturgical discipline and advance more spiritually substantive pastoral practice on the part of those who lead the worship of the Church. Otherwise, some of the factors that created the traditionalist movement in the first place will be exacerbated. The pre-conciliar liturgy – and the restora-tionist agenda now promoting it – have much to teach the Church today, even if the formal aspects of that agenda cannot be substantially embraced.

Regarding the agenda of reforming the reform – at least in its present high-profile expressions – I think it unrealistic to imagine that it will have much significant short-term success. In my opinion, the bishops of the English-speaking world are not likely to muster noticeable enthusiasm for the advancement of this agenda, and I cannot imagine that the Holy See would undertake or approve such a programme due to its uncertain outcome. Beyond this, some elements of the agenda as outlined by Harrison would be quite unacceptable to even moderately 'conservative' liturgical voices – especially the desire to curtail new eucharistic prayers, reduce women's roles in liturgical ministries and refuse any consideration of adaptation in the area of gender language. This agenda seems too severe in its specific proposals and inadequately appreciative of the revised liturgical order.

An argument can be made in retrospect that greater continuity should have been maintained between the Missal of 1962 (and its 1965 and 1967 revisions) and the distinctly different order of Mass promulgated in 1969. But it would be unwise to marginalise the rite we now have in favour of some modification of the Mass as it was before the Council. The creation of yet another rite such as Harrison proposes would, in my opinion, only add to present confusion and instability. Yet, the recovery of some elements from the pre-conciliar liturgy should not be ruled out in any further modification of the present Mass. The reform of the reform programme has some important lessons to teach, especially concerning the dangers of discontinuity in liturgical reform and undue haste in any further round of revisions. As the agenda of reforming the reform matures, it will surely have important contributions to make in discussions about the future of the Roman liturgy. Those who espouse the recatholicisation agenda are likely to consider those contributions respectfully. It would be unwise for the official and the recatholicisation agendas to refuse to take account of the important warning signalled by the publication and widespread popular reception of Gamber's book.[80]

The inculturation agenda can, as I pointed out, claim legitimacy by reference to Articles 37–40 of the Constitution on the Sacred Liturgy, and I have no doubt that this programme needs to be carried through, especially in relation to non-Western cultures, as well as to the traditional cultures of the West – including, in the United States, Hispanics, Native Americans, Asians and African-Americans. As already indicated, this agenda rightly finds support in the present thinking of the Holy See regarding the ongoing evangelisation of cultures.[81]

The possibility of new expressions of liturgical catholicity should be explored and advanced. On this project a creative and productive dialogue between the recatholicisation and inculturation agendas is possible. Yet, in my opinion, the inculturation agenda has not yet matured, even theoretically. The practical difficulties of carrying out appropriate adaptation of rites, both in Western and non-Western cultures, have already proved daunting. The possibility of the dissolution of the Roman liturgy and the liturgical corruption of the Church's worship are very real. Indeed, in my opinion, the most severe problems that exist in the Church's liturgical life today, especially in the United States, are the result of an unfortunate practical adaptation of liturgy to American popular culture.[82] These problems include the trivialisation of rites and symbols, the ascendancy of an entertainment and therapeutic ethos in liturgical celebration, an exaggerated, neo-clericalist style of priestly presidency and an individualistic and consumerist spirituality.[83] What Aidan Kavanagh has often spoken of as the 'embourgeoisement' of the liturgy, that is, its adaptation in the West to liberal middle-class concerns, is a matter requiring critical evaluation.[84] The most troublesome challenges facing ongoing liturgical renewal over the next twenty-five years will be, as I envisage them, in the area of inculturation. Accordingly, the greatest of caution is in order as more adequate theologies of the relationship between Church and cultures are developed.[85]

The recatholicising agenda summarised and advocated in this essay has undoubted weaknesses. It could be accused, in its turn, of settling in an unprincipled manner for the liturgical books published since the Second Vatican Council; of extrapolating from the new rites a spirituality that they do not possess; and of practising a simple 'politics of moderation' regarding the present configuration of liturgical controversies. On the first point, the recatholicisation agenda recognises that the liturgical books the Church now possesses were not easily devised; they represent a massive investment of time, talent and financial resources; and they are weighted with as providential a character as that properly ascribed to the Second Vatican Council. There is the further related conviction of this agenda group that stability in ritual order and authentic popular ownership of the liturgy are values of the highest importance and should not be compromised for excessively theoretical reasons. The revised liturgical order is far from perfect; but it was achieved at a high and difficult cost and thus merits ongoing respect on the part of the whole Church.

Does the recatholicisation agenda extrapolate from or impose upon the revised liturgy a spiritual ethos that it does not possess? Are the reformed rites capable of bearing the Catholic expressivity I have described? I would answer, yes. This conviction derives from my actual observation and experience as a parish priest. When celebrated with attentiveness to ritual and text, with spiritual profundity, nobility and solemnity, with well-formed ministerial leadership, and with rich musical, artistic and architectural elaboration, the present liturgy is pastorally most edifying and deeply expressive of Catholic fullness. I would, of course, readily admit that liturgical celebration of the kind I have in mind is not often encountered today and that the liturgy of Catholicism as currently practised in most parishes does not adequately display the Catholic vision I have described. However, where an impoverished liturgical practice is in operation, it will not be resolved by further structural revisions of the liturgy, but only by the intense spiritual renewal that this essay proposes.

The operation of a 'politics of moderation' in this agenda can be readily admitted, if what is in mind is the necessity of the development of a broad consensus regarding liturgical matters and an ecclesial unity inclusive of the legitimate aspirations of the various agendas described in this essay. The agenda of recatholicisation has, in my opinion, much to offer in reaching across the divides that currently exist and which require genuine reconciliation before any further reform of the liturgy is wisely undertaken.

Notes

1   My use of the term 'agenda' generally invokes the methodologies of models, paradigms and typologies that have become a familiar feature of modern theology. An 'agenda' may be understood as the *practical* outworking of a *conceptual* model, paradigm or typology.

2   See Avery Dulles, *Models of the Church* (Garden City, NY: Doubleday, 1974); *Models of Revelation* (Garden City, NY: Doubleday, 1985).

3   See, for instance, Frederick R. McManus (ed.), *Thirty Years of Liturgical Renewal: Statements of the Bishops' Committee on the Liturgy* (Washington, DC: United States Catholic Conference, 1987).

4   The most useful and comprehensive published source for the official agenda in relation to the Holy See is *Documents on the Liturgy 1963–1979: Conciliar, Papal, and Curial Texts* (Collegeville, MN: Liturgical Press, 1982).

5   Annibale Bugnini, *The Reform of the Liturgy 1948–1975*, trans. Matthew J. O'Connell (Collegeville, MN: Liturgical Press, 1990).

6   See the chapter entitled 'Fundamental Principles' in ibid., pp. 39–48; also Kathleen Hughes, 'Overview of the Constitution on the Sacred Liturgy', in *The Liturgy Documents: A Parish Resource* (Chicago, IL: Liturgy Training Publications, 1991), pp. 2–6.

7   Beginning with the *motu proprio* on the Sacred Liturgy (*Sacram Liturgiam*) of 25 January 1964, the process of evolution may be traced through the Instructions on the Proper Implementation of the Constitution on the Sacred Liturgy issued in 1964, 1967 and 1970, as well as through the many specific decrees and official communications of that period. See the chapter entitled 'Implementation of the Constitution on the Sacred Liturgy' in R. Kevin Seasoltz, *New Liturgy, New Laws* (Collegeville, MN: Liturgical Press, 1980), pp. 26–37.

8   See the commentary on this point in Austin Flannery (ed.), *Vatican Council II: The Conciliar and Post-Conciliar Documents* (Collegeville, MN: Liturgical Press, 1975), p. 39.

9   No. 1; text in *Documents on the Liturgy 1963–1979*, p. 284. (See n. 4 above.)

10 On the work of ICEL, see John R. Page, 'Liturgical Texts in English', in Peter E. Fink (ed.), *The New Dictionary of Sacramental Worship* (Collegeville, MN: Liturgical Press, 1990), pp. 715–21; Frederick R. McManus, 'ICEL: The First Years', in Peter C. Finn and James M. Schellman (eds.), *Shaping English Liturgy: Studies in Honor of Archbishop Denis Hurley* (Washington, DC: Pastoral Press, 1990), pp. 433–59. Noteworthy also are the essays in the latter volume by H. Kathleen Hughes and John R. Page.

11 See the 3 May 1996 address of Pope John Paul II to the plenary assembly of the Congregation for Divine Worship and the Discipline of the Sacraments; text in Bishops' Committee on the Liturgy *Newsletter* 32 (May 1996), pp. 17–19.

12   See, for instance, Adrien Nocent, *A Rereading of the Renewed Liturgy*, trans.
      Mary M. Misrahi (Collegeville, MN: Liturgical Press, 1994). See, more
      generally, Carl A. Last (ed.), *Remembering the Future: Vatican II and
      Tomorrow's Liturgical Agenda* (New York: Paulist Press, 1983).

13   The publications of Michael Davies are the most popular and widely used
      in English-speaking restorationist circles. See *Liturgical Revolution. Volume
      I: Cranmer's Godly Order* (Kansas City, MO: Angelus Press, 1976); *Liturgical
      Revolution. Volume II: Pope John's Council* (New Rochelle, NY: Arlington
      House, 1977); *Liturgical Revolution. Volume III: Pope Paul's New Mass* (Kansas
      City, MO: Angelus Press, 1980); *The New Mass* (Kansas City, MO: Angelus
      Press, 1985); *The Legal Status of the Tridentine Mass* (Dickinson, TX: Angelus
      Press, 1992); *The Roman Rite Destroyed* (Kansas City, MO: Angelus Press,
      1992); *Liturgical Shipwreck: 25 Years of the New Mass* (Rockford, IL: Tan
      Books, 1995); *On Communion in the Hand and Similar Frauds* (St Paul, MN:
      Remnant Press, n.d.).

14   For a 'conservative' defence of the Mass of 1969 against its critics, see
      James Likoudis and Kenneth D. Whitehead, *The Pope, the Council, and the
      Mass: Answers to Questions the 'Traditionalists' are Asking* (West Hanover,
      MA: Christopher Publishing House, 1981).

15   The recent reissue of what was known as the 'Ottaviani Intervention' – a
      programme led by Cardinal Alfredo Ottaviani on behalf of Cardinal
      Antonio Bacci and a group of Roman theologians in 1969 – against certain
      proposals for liturgical reform – has reopened in some circles the debate
      about 'politics' surrounding the promulgation of the Mass of 1969. See
      The Ottaviani Intervention: Short Critical Study of the New Order of Mass, with a
      new translation and preface by Anthony Cekada (Rockford, IL: Tan Books,
      1992).

16   See Patrick H. Omlor, *Questioning the Validity* (Reno, NV: Athanasius Press,
      1969); William Strojie, *The New Mass Invalid Because of Defect of Intention*
      (Sheridan, OR: n.p., 1972); James Wathen, *The Great Sacrilege* (Rockford,
      IL: Tan Books, 1971).

17   For an overview of the various groupings within the restorationist category
      and the history of their development in the United States after the Second
      Vatican Council, see the essay by William D. Dinges, '"We Are What You
      Were": Roman Catholic Traditionalism in America', in Mary Jo Weaver
      and R. Scott Appleby (eds.), *Being Right: Conservative Catholics in America*
      (Bloomington, IN: Indiana University Press, 1995), pp. 241–69.

18   Latin Liturgy Association *Newsletter* 59 (Dec. 1995), p. 10.

19   Ibid.

20   Ibid.

21   Ibid.

22   Texts in *Origins* 14:19 (24 Oct. 1984), p. 290; 18:10 (4 Aug. 1988), pp.
      149–52.

23   See the essays by Jeffrey Rubin entitled 'Traditional Monastic Revival' and
     'Louder than Words', in *Latin Mass Revival: Chronicle of a Catholic Reform*
     (Fort Collins, CO: Roman Catholic Books, 1996), pp. 47–59; pp. 128–30.

24   See Dinges, '"We Are What You Were"', p. 268, n. 74.

25   Raymond E. Brown, *Biblical Reflections on Crises Facing the Church* (New
     York: Paulist Press, 1975), pp. 24–27.

26   See the following reports: 'Scholars Meet in France', *Precious Blood Banner*,
     Oct. 1995, p. 4; 'Liturgy in Critical Focus', *The Tablet*, 16 Nov. 1996, p. 519.

27   See Dinges, '"We Are What You Were"', p. 242.

28   A 1990 Gallup poll indicated that the percentages of Catholics who, if it
     were available, would attend the traditional Latin Mass were as follows: 8%
     always; 17% frequently, 51% occasionally. See *Latin Mass Revival*, p. 5.

29   It should be noted that Latin Mass groups or organisations are not always
     in favour of or actively committed to the restoration of the Tridentine
     Mass. Some groups simply espouse the more frequent use of Latin in the
     celebration of the 1969 Mass. In this category are the St Gregory
     Foundation for Latin Liturgy in the United States and the Association for
     Latin Liturgy in England.

30   Klaus Gamber, *The Reform of the Roman Liturgy: Its Problems and Background*,
     trans. Klaus D. Grimm (San Juan Capistrano, CA: Una Voce Press, 1993).

31   Ibid., p. 3.

32   Ibid., p. xii.

33   Public Letter of 29 June 1995; emphasis in original.

34   Text from Flannery (ed.), *Vatican Council II*, 10. The immediate inspiration
     for the foundation of Adoremus was the Apostolic Letter of Pope John
     Paul II, 'On the 25th Anniversary of the Constitution on the Sacred
     Liturgy' (4 Dec. 1988), which stated: 'For the work of translation, as well
     as for the wider implications of liturgical renewal for whole countries,
     each Episcopal Conference was required to establish a National Commis-
     sion and ensure the collaboration of experts in the various sectors of
     liturgical and pastoral practice. The time has come to evaluate this
     Commission, its past activity, both the positive and negative aspects, and
     the guidelines and the help which it has received from the Episcopal
     Conference regarding its composition and activity' (no. 20). Text available
     from Washington, DC: United States Catholic Conference, 1989. See also:
     'About Adoremus: A Statement of its Missions, Goals and Principles',
     Adoremus Bulletin, Nov. 1995, p. 2; 'Adoremus – Society for the Renewal of
     Sacred Liturgy', *Voices* [Women for Faith and Family], June 1996, p. 6;
     Philip F. Lawler, 'A Reform of the Reform?', *The Catholic World Report*,
     Aug.–Sept. 1996, pp. 40–42.

35   Brian W. Harrison, 'What Do We Do Now? Part III: The Gamber Proposal
     as Long-Term Solution', *Adoremus Bulletin*, Jan. 1996, p. 1; emphasis in
     original. The other parts of this essay are 'The Crisis in Eucharistic Faith:

Implications for Post-Vatican II Reform', *Adoremus Bulletin*, Nov. 1995, pp. 1, 8; 'Planning a "Reform of the Reform". Part II: Some Inadequate Solutions to the Eucharistic Liturgy Crisis', *Adoremus Bulletin*, Dec. 1995, pp. 1, 8. Significantly, the 'Reform of the Reform' for which Harrison calls involves an explicit rejection of the 'Traditionalist Proposal', that is, the view that the solution to the present crisis in Catholic worship is simply the restoration of the Mass as it was before the Council ('Planning a "Reform of the Reform"', p. 8).

36 Harrison, 'Planning a "Reform of the Reform"', p. 8.

37 Harrison, 'What Do We Do Now', *passim*. Harrison's proposal regarding the exclusive use of men in lay service in the liturgy is developed at greater length in '"*Fluctuationes Rhythmicae*": The New Feminist Face of the Roman Liturgy', *The Latin Mass*, Fall 1995, pp. 42–49.

38 Aidan Nichols, *Looking at the Liturgy: A Critical View of its Contemporary Form* (San Francisco, CA: Ignatius Press, 1996). Nichols proposes that the Mass of 1969 be redesignated as a *ritus communis* with multiple purposes, including: providing the basis for developing new ritual families in non-Western areas of the Church; serving as a rite for Anglicans and Lutherans wishing to join the Church in some corporate manner; and continuing in use 'in those parishes and religious communities of the Latin church that do not wish to recover the historical and spiritual patrimony of the Latin rite in a fuller form' (p. 122). See also James Hitchcock, *Recovery of the Sacred. Reforming the Reformed Liturgy* (San Francisco, CA: Ignatius Press, 1995); this is a reprint with a new preface of a work first published in 1974.

39 See Thomas J. Nash, 'Adoremus Seeks to Restore a Sense of the Sacred in the Mass', *Lay Witness*, May 1996, p. 20.

40 In the mission statement of Adoremus, the following question is posed: 'Is Adoremus promoting a more careful observance of the liturgical norms approved since the Council?' The answer is, 'Yes, but not as our ultimate goal. With Pope John Paul II, we believe that even some of the changes approved since the Council need to be reviewed and measured against a deeper understanding of the Council's teaching' (*Adoremus Bulletin*, Nov. 1995, p. 2). The same mission statement responds to the question, 'Is Adoremus seeking a restoration of the pre-conciliar liturgy?' as follows: 'No. We do not think that a simple return to the pre-conciliar liturgy will further the reforms legitimately mandated by the Second Vatican Council' (ibid.).

41 On this point, see Article 53 of the 1994 Instruction of the Vatican Congregation for Divine Worship and the Discipline of the Sacraments, entitled 'Inculturation and the Roman Liturgy', which states: 'The first significant measure of inculturation is the translation of liturgical books into the language of the people' (text in *Origins* 23:43 (14 Apr. 1994), p. 745, pp. 747–56). See also Andrew Borello, 'The Contextualization of Liturgy and Especially Liturgical Texts: The Tension

Between the Universality of the Liturgy and the Specific Situation of the Local Celebrating Community' and Paul Puthanangady, 'Cultural Elements in Liturgical Prayers', both in Finn and Schellman (eds.), *Shaping English Liturgy*, pp. 301–26, pp. 327–40; Stephen M. Beall, 'Translation and Inculturation in the Catholic Church', *Adoremus Bulletin*, Oct. 1996, pp. 1, 6.

42 See the various essays in David Power and Herman Schmidt (eds.), *Liturgy and Cultural Religious Traditions*, Concilium 102 (New York: Seabury Press, 1977); Mary Collins and David Power (eds.), *Liturgy: A Creative Tradition*, Concilium 162 (New York: Seabury Press, 1983). See also David N. Power, *Worship: Culture and Theology* (Washington, DC: Pastoral Press, 1990); James Empereur, *Worship: Exploring the Sacred* (Washington, DC: Pastoral Press, 1987).

43 Papers related to the conference were published in *Theological Studies* 35:2 (1974). In that volume, see Walter J. Burghardt, 'A Theologian's Challenge to Liturgy', pp. 233–48; Langdon Gilkey, 'Symbols, Meaning and Divine Presence', pp. 249–67; James F. White, 'Worship and Culture: Mirror or Beacon?', pp. 288–301; John Gallen, 'American Liturgy: A Theological Locus', pp. 302–11. See also Mary Collins, 'Liturgy in America: The Scottsdale Conference', *Worship* 48 (1974), pp. 66–80.

44 On the broader theological-cultural features of this challenge see M. Francis Mannion, 'Evangelization and American Ethnicity', in *Proceedings from the Seventeenth Convention of the Fellowship of Catholic Scholars* (Corpus Christi, TX: 1994), pp. 145–92.

45 A comprehensive introduction to this matter is provided in *Liturgy Digest* 1:2 (1994), pp. 78–185. See also National Conference of Catholic Bishops, *Criteria for the Evaluation of Inclusive Language Translations of Scriptural Texts Prepared for Liturgical Use* (Washington, DC: United States Catholic Conference, 1990); Ronald D. Witherup, *A Liturgist's Guide to Inclusive Language* (Collegeville, MN: Liturgical Press, 1996); Kathleen Hughes, 'Inclusive Language Revisited', *Chicago Studies* 35 (1996), pp. 115–27; Janet Walton, 'Feminism and the Liturgy', in Fink (ed.), *The New Dictionary of Sacramental Worship*, pp. 468–73; the essays 'Inclusive Language: A Cultural and Theological Question' and 'Naming God in Public Prayer' in Mary Collins, *Worship: Renewal to Practice* (Washington, DC: Pastoral Press, 1987), pp. 197–214; pp. 215–29.

46 See the various essays and useful bibliography provided in J. Frank Henderson, Kathleen Quinn and Stephen Larson, *Liturgy, Justice and the Reign of God: Interpretating Vision and Practice* (New York: Paulist Press, 1989); the essays by Elisabeth Schüssler Fiorenza, Enrique Dussel and Diann Neu in Mary Collins and David Power (eds.), *Can We Always Celebrate the Eucharist?* Concilium, p. 152 (New York: Seabury Press, 1982); the essay entitled 'The Liberation Model of Liturgical Theology' in Empereur, *Worship: Exploring the Sacred*, pp. 97–118. Tissa Balasuriya, *The Eucharist and*

Human Liberation (Maryknoll, NY: Orbis Books, 1979) has been particularly influential on the reconstructive role of liberation themes on liturgical practice.

47   Text in Flannery (ed.), *Vatican Council*, p. 13.

48   Ibid.

49   Ibid., p. 14.

50   Ibid.

51   See Anscar J. Chupungco, *Cultural Adaptation of the Liturgy* (New York: Paulist Press, 1982); *Liturgies of the Future: The Process and Methods of Inculturation* (New York: Paulist Press, 1989); *Liturgical Inculturation: Sacramentals, Religiosity, and Catechesis* (Collegeville, MN: Liturgical Press, 1992).

52   See, for example, the volumes produced in the Alternative Futures for Worship Series, general ed. Bernard J. Lee (Collegeville, MN: Liturgical Press, 1987). Noteworthy is the 'Introduction to the Series' by Lee in vol. 1: *General Introduction*, ed. Regis A. Duffy, pp. 9–28.

53   This agenda title is neither meant to suggest that the other positions are not Catholic, nor to invoke the arguments of some critics that Catholic liturgy has suffered a 'Protestantising' process since the Second Vatican Council. Indeed, some important sources for liturgical recatholicisation are, as I shall demonstrate, drawn from Orthodox, Anglican and Reformed sources.

54   Avery Dulles, *The Catholicity of the Church* (Oxford: Clarendon Press, 1985); see also the essay entitled 'The Meaning of Catholicism: Adventures of an Idea' in Avery Dulles, *The Reshaping of Catholicism. Current Challenges in the Theology of the Church* (San Francisco, CA: Harper & Row, 1988), pp. 51–74. Page references embedded in the text refer to the 1985 book.

55   See also Henri de Lubac, *Catholicism: Christ and the Common Destiny of Man*, trans. Lancelot C. Sheppard and Sister Elizabeth Englund, new edn. (San Francisco, CA: Ignatius Press, 1988); *The Splendour of the Church*, trans. Michael Mason (Glen Rock, NJ: Paulist Press, 1963); Karl Adam, *The Spirit of Catholicism*, trans. Justin McCann (London: Sheed & Ward, 1934); Wolfgang Beinert, *Um das dritte Kirchenattribut*, 2 vols. (Essen: Ludgerus-Verlag, 1964); Ian Ker, *Newman and the Fullness of Christianity* (Edinburgh: T&T Clark, 1993), esp. chaps. 6 and 7. A more popular treatment of this theme is found in Richard P. McBrien, *Catholicism*, revised edn. (San Francisco, CA: Harper, 1994), esp. pp. 3–17; and in Robert P. Imbelli, 'Vatican II: Twenty Years Later', *Commonweal*, 8 Oct. 1982, pp. 522–26.

56   On various conceptions of ethos in relation to Christian worship, see Chacko Aerath, *Liturgy and Ethos: A Study Based on the Malankara Liturgy of Marriage* (Rome: Mar Yogam, 1995).

57   For a positive, if not uncritical, evaluation of the current translation work of ICEL, see Eamon Duffy's essay in this volume. The necessity of producing translations faithful to the theological richness of the

Roman Rite is examined in Jeremy Driscoll, 'Deepening the Theological Dimensions of Liturgical Studies', *Communio* 23 (1996), pp.
508–23. CREDO: A Society for Catholic Priests Dedicated to Faithful
Translation of the Liturgy seeks not only to foster accurate and doctrinally
adequate translations but to ensure a language of worship that fosters
dignity and beauty in liturgical celebration.

58 For sociologist David Martin, 'rite' depends for success on 'rote', on a
strongly internalised familiarity with the verbal and ritual structures on
the part of liturgical participants. See *The Breaking of the Image: A Sociology
of Christian Theory and Practice* (Oxford: Basil Blackwell, 1985), esp. pp. 81–
102.

59 See M. Francis Mannion, 'Sunday in Modern America: A Cultural
Perspective', *Chicago Studies* 29 (1990), pp. 224–35, esp. pp. 231–32.

60 See Walter Kasper, 'The Council's Vision for a Renewal of the Church',
Communio 17 (1990), pp. 484–85. In the address to the Plenary Assembly
of the Congregation for Divine Worship and the Discipline of the
Sacraments, Pope John Paul II emphasised the ideal of a *spiritual* renewal
of the liturgy: 'It was obvious that the spirit of the liturgy could not be
restored by means of a mere reform. A true, profound liturgical renewal
was necessary. In fact a "spirit" intrinsically linked with liturgical "actions"
can reside only in the "human agents" of the liturgy, who are called to
"exercise Christ's priestly office". However, this does not mean that one
should neglect the forms in which Christ's priesthood is expressed and
exercised, those "outward signs" which the liturgy must take into
consideration' (text in Bishops' Committee on the Liturgy *Newsletter* 32
(May 1996), pp. 17–18).

61 If excessive liturgical institutionalism may be inhospitable to the mystical
and the spiritual, a spirituality or mysticism detached from the liturgy is
equally troublesome. The works of Louis Bouyer are particularly important
in integrating the mystical and the sacramental features of Christian life.
See *The Christian Mystery: From Pagan Myth to Christian Mysticism*, trans. Illtyd
Trethowan (Petersham, MA: St Bede's Publications, 1990); *Rite and Man:
Natural Sacredness and Christian Liturgy*, trans. M. Joseph Costelloe
(University of Notre Dame Press, 1963); also Erasmo Leiva-Merikakis,
'Louis Bouyer the Theologian', *Communio* 16 (1989), pp. 257–82. Eastern
Christianity may be proposed as exemplary on the integration of the
mystical and the sacramental. See, for instance, Vladimir Lossky, *The
Mystical Theology of the Eastern Church* (Crestwood, NJ: St Vladimir's
Seminary Press, 1976). See also Frans Josef van Beeck, *Catholic Identity after
Vatican II: Three Types of Faith in the One Church* (Chicago, IL: Loyola
University Press, 1985), esp. chap. 3.

62 Rudolf Otto, *The Idea of the Holy: An Inquiry into the Non-Rational Factor
in the Idea of the Divine and its Relation to the Rational*, trans. John W.
Harvey (New York: Oxford University Press, 1923); Gerardus van der
Leeuw, *Religion in Essence and Manifestation*, trans. J. E. Turner (New York:

Harper & Row, 1963). Eliade's extensive writings in this area are sum-marised in the chapter entitled 'The Reality of the Sacred: Mircea Eliade' in Daniel L. Pals, *Seven Theories of Religion* (New York: Oxford University Press, 1996), pp. 158–97. See also Josef Pieper, *In Search of the Sacred: Contributions to an Answer*, trans. Lothar Krauth (San Francisco, CA: Ignatius Press, 1991).

63   See Patrick Regan, 'Pneumatological and Eschatological Aspects of Liturgical Celebrations', *Worship* 51 (1977), pp. 332–50; the chapter entitled 'Spirit' in Geoffrey Wainwright, *Doxology: The Praise of God in Worship, Doctrine and Life* (New York: Oxford University Press, 1980), pp. 87–117; Edward J. Kilmartin, *Christian Liturgy: Theology and Practice. I: Systematic Theology of Liturgy* (Kansas: MO: Sheed & Ward, 1988), and 'A Modern Approach to the Word of God and Sacraments of Christ. Perspectives and Principles', in Francis A. Eigo (ed.), *The Sacraments: God's Love and Mercy Actualized* (Villanova, PA: Villanova University Press, 1979), pp. 59–109; Aidan Kavanagh, 'Liturgy and Ecclesial Consciousness', *Studia Liturgica* 15 (1982–83), pp. 2–17; Peter C. Sanders, 'Pneumatology in the Sacramental Theologies of Geoffrey Wainwright, Jean Corbon and Edward Kilmartin', *Worship* 68 (1994), pp. 332–52.

64   For a valuable introduction to this theme, see the special issue of *Liturgy Digest* 3:1 (1996), esp. pp. 72ff. See also Don E. Saliers, 'Liturgical Aesthetics', in Fink (ed.), *The New Dictionary of Sacramental Worship*, pp. 30–39; Nicholas Wolterstorff, *Art in Action: Toward a Christian Aesthetic* (Grand Rapids, MI: Eerdmans, 1980); Frank Burch Brown, *Religious Aesthetics: A Theological Study of Making and Meaning* (Princeton University Press, 1989).

65   See Gordon Jeanes, 'Liturgy and Ceremonial', in Paul Bradshaw and Bryan Spinks (eds.), *Liturgy in Dialogue: Essays in Memory of Ronald Jasper* (Collegeville, MN: Liturgical Press, 1993), pp. 9–27; Hugh Wybrew, 'Ceremonial', in Cheslyn Jones, Geoffrey Wainwright, Edward Yarnold and Paul Bradshaw (eds.), *The Study of Liturgy*, revised edn. (New York: Oxford University Press, 1992), pp. 485–93; Richard G. Cippola, 'Ceremonial and the Tacit Dimension', *Worship* 47 (1973), pp. 398–404. On the uses of ritual studies in liturgiology, see *Liturgy Digest* 1:1 (1993); Mark Searle, 'Ritual', in Jones *et al.* (eds.), *The Study of Liturgy*, pp. 51–58. On anti-ritual bias, see Margaret Mead, *Twentieth-Century Faith: Hope and Survival* (New York: Harper, 1978), pp. 125–26; Roger Grainger, *The Language of the Rite* (London: Darton, Longman & Todd, 1974), pp. 23–106; Mary Douglas, *Natural Symbols: Explorations in Cosmology* (Harmondsworth: Penguin Books, 1973), esp. pp. 19–39.

66   *Catechism of the Catholic Church*, paragraphs 1091, 1116 (New York: Catholic Book Publishing Co., 1994), pp. 283, 289.

67   Recent writings on the eschatological character of worship include Mary M. Schaefer, 'Heavenly and Earthly Liturgies: Patristic Prototypes, Medieval Perspectives and a Contemporary Application', *Worship* 70 (1996), pp. 482–505; Jean-Pierre Ruiz, 'The Apocalypse of John and

Contemporary Roman Catholic Liturgy', *Worship* 68 (1994), pp. 482–504; Geoffrey Wainwright, 'The Church as a Worshipping Community', *Pro Ecclesia* 4 (1993), pp. 56–67. See also Laurence Hull Stookey, *Eucharist: Christ's Feast with the Church* (Nashville, TN: Abingdon Press, 1993); Don E. Saliers, *Worship as Theology: Foretaste of Divine Glory* (Nashville, TN: Abingdon Press, 1994).

68 This development may be traced to a tendency to reinterpret the Constitution on the Sacred Liturgy through the hermeneutical structure provided by features of the conciliar Constitution on the Church in the Modern World approved in 1965. For an advocacy of this development, see the chapters entitled 'Two Models of Christian Worship' and 'Liturgical Spirituality, Conciliar Foundations', in Shawn Madigan, *Spirituality Rooted in Liturgy* (Washington, DC: Pastoral Press, 1988), pp. 89–115, 117–37.

69 The eschatological and cosmic dimensions of worship are expressively interrelated in the new Catechism of the Catholic Church. In answer to the question 'Who celebrates the liturgy?' the following answer is given: 'These are the ones who take part in the service of the praise of God and the fulfilment of his plan: the heavenly powers, all creation (the four living beings), the servants of the Old and New Covenants (the twenty-four elders), the new People of God (the one hundred and forty-four thousand), especially the martyrs, "slain for the word of God", and the all-holy Mother of God (the Woman), the Bride of the Lamb, and finally "a great multitude which no one could number, from every nation, from all tribes, and peoples and tongues"' (paragraph 1138; text in *Catechism of the Catholic Church*, p. 295). See also Louis Bouyer, *Cosmos: The World and the Glory of God*, trans. Pierre de Fontnouvelle (Petersham, MA: St Bede's Publications, 1988); Pope John Paul II, Apostolic Letter: 'Orientale Lumen', paragraph 11; text in *Origins* 25:1 (18 May 1995), p. 7; the chapter entitled 'The Cosmic Setting of Salvation', in Aidan Nichols, *Epiphany: A Theological Introduction to Catholicism* (Collegeville, MN: Liturgical Press, 1996), pp. 368–90. For Dulles, the Trinity is the originating principle of cosmic theology (see *The Catholicity of the Church*, esp. pp. 34–39).

70 See M. Francis Mannion, 'Catholic Worship and the Dynamics of Congregationalism', *Chicago Studies* 33 (1994), pp. 57–66.

71 Classic works in this area eminently worthy of reconsideration include Josef Pieper, *In Tune with the World: A Theory of Festivity*, trans. Richard and Clara Winston (Chicago, IL: Franciscan Herald Press, 1973); Romano Guardini, *The Spirit of the Liturgy*, trans. Ada Lane (London: Sheed & Ward, 1937), esp. pp. 95–106; Hugo Rahner, *Man at Play or Did You Ever Practice Eutrapelia?*, trans. Brian Battershaw and Edward Quinn (London: Burns & Oates, 1965). See also Wainwright, *Doxology*; Daniel W. Hardy and David F. Ford, *Jubilate: Theology in Praise* (London: Darton, Longman & Todd, 1984); Hughes Oliphant Old, *Themes and Variations for a Christian Doxology*

(Grand Rapids, MI: Eerdmans, 1992); Jürgen Moltmann, *Theology and Joy*, trans. Richard Ulrich (London: SCM Press, 1973). On the contemplative aspects of the liturgy, see Jacques and Raïssa Maritain, *Liturgy and Contemplation*, trans. Joseph W. Evans (New York: P. J. Kenedy & Sons, 1960); more recently, Max Thurian, 'The Liturgy and Contemplation', *L'Osservatore Romano* (English edn.), no. 30 (24 July 1996), pp. 2, 4.

72   A classic statement on the ability of the modern person to participate authentically in 'the liturgical act' is found in Romano Guardini, 'Liturgical Worship and Modern Man', a letter to the 1964 Mainz Liturgical Congress, *Doctrine and Life*, Sept. 1964, pp. 426–32.

73   On liturgical music, see *The Snowbird Statement on Catholic Liturgical Music* (Salt Lake City, UT: Madeleine Institute, 1995); M. Francis Mannion, 'Paradigms in American Catholic Church Music', *Worship* 70 (1996), pp. 101–28. On liturgical art and architecture, see Dennis McNally, *Sacred Space: An Aesthetic for the Liturgical Environment* (Bristol, IN: Wyndham Hall Press, 1985); M. Francis Mannion, 'Toward a New Era in Liturgical Architecture' (forthcoming, *Liturgical Ministry*, Fall 1997).

74   Eamon Duffy, *The Stripping of the Altars: Traditional Religion in England, 1400–1580* (New Haven, CT: Yale University Press, 1992); 'Lay Appropriation of the Sacraments in the Later Middle Ages', *New Blackfriars* 77 (1996), pp. 53–68. See also Paul Bradshaw, 'The Liturgical Use and Abuse of Patristics', in Kenneth Stevenson (ed.), *Liturgy Reshaped* (London: SPCK, 1982), pp. 134–45; Dulles, *The Catholicity of the Church*, pp. 94–103.

75   New editions of classic works from the liturgical movement before the Second Vatican Council are long overdue. Robert A. Krieg points out that the writings of Romano Guardini are today no longer well known; yet he worries about 'a risk involved in publishing Guardini's works anew in North America today'. The risk is that Guardini could be 'misconstrued now to support a neoconservative or "restorationist" agenda' in liturgical matters ('North American Catholics' Reception of Romano Guardini's Writings', in Robert A. Krieg (ed.), *Romano Guardini: Proclaiming the Sacred in a Modern World* (Chicago, IL: Liturgy Training Publications, 1995, p. 55). The assumption here is that Guardini and scholars like him would be supportive of the progressive liturgical agenda of the 1990s. Such assumptions defy verification.

76   Von Balthasar's corpus of explicit writings on liturgy and the sacraments is relatively small. However, according to Gerald O'Collins, the whole character of his theology is one for which prayer and worship form the context (*Retrieving Fundamental Theology: The Three Styles of Contemporary Theology* (Mahwah, NJ: Paulist Press, 1993), p. 10 and *passim*). The following writings of von Balthasar on liturgical topics are noteworthy: the essay entitled 'Liturgy and Awe', in *Explorations in Theology II: Spouse of the Word*, trans. A. V. Littledale with Alexander Dru (San Francisco, CA: Ignatius Press, 1991), pp. 461–72; the section entitled 'The Eucharistic Cult', in *The Glory of the Lord: A Theological Aesthetics. Volume I: Seeing the*

Form, trans. Erasmo Leiva-Merikakis (San Francisco, CA: Ignatius Press, 1982), pp. 571–75; 'The Grandeur of the Liturgy', *Communio* 4 (1978), pp. 344–51; the entries entitled 'The Eucharistic Self-Giving of Jesus' and 'The Mass as Meal and Sacrifice' in Medard Kehl and Werner Löser (eds.), *The Von Balthasar Reader*, trans. Robert J. Daly and Fred Lawrence (New York: Crossroad, 1982), pp. 282–88; the essay entitled 'The Worthiness of the Liturgy', in *New Elucidations*, trans. Sister Mary Theresilde Skerry (San Francisco, CA: Ignatius Press, 1986), pp. 127–40; *Mysterium Paschale: The Mystery of Easter*, trans. Aidan Nichols (Grand Rapids, MI: William B. Eerdmans, 1994). See also Mark Miller, 'The Sacramental Theology of Hans Urs von Balthasar', *Worship* 64 (1990), pp. 48–66.

77 Useful introductions to Eastern liturgical tradition written from Western perspectives include Thomas Fisch (ed.), *Liturgy and Tradition: Theological Reflections of Alexander Schmemann* (Crestwood, NY: St Vladimir's Seminary Press, 1990); Aidan Nichols, *Light from the East: Authors and Themes in Orthodox Theology* (London: Sheed & Ward, 1995); Hans-Joachim Schulz, *The Byzantine Liturgy: Symbolic Structure and Faith Expressions*, trans. Matthew J. O'Connell (New York: Pueblo Publishing Company, 1986); Boniface Luykx, *Theological Foundations of the Byzantine Liturgy* (Redwood, CA: Holy Transfiguration Monastery, 1994); Jean Corbon, *The Wellspring of Worship*, trans. Matthew J. O'Connell (New York: Paulist Press, 1988); Robert Taft, *Beyond East and West: Problems in Liturgical Understanding* (Washington, DC: Pastoral Press, 1984); Joan L. Roccasalvo, *The Eastern Catholic Churches: An Introduction to their Worship and Spirituality*, American Essays in Liturgy (Collegeville, MN: Liturgical Press, 1992).

78 A useful introduction to the criticisms of liturgical reform by Catholic anthropologists Mary Douglas, Victor Turner and Kieran Flanagan is provided in Nichols, *Looking at the Liturgy*, chap. 2. See also Aidan Kavanagh, 'Liturgy (*Sacrosanctum Concilium*)', in Adrian Hastings (ed.), *Modern Catholicism: Vatican II and After* (New York: Oxford University Press, 1991), pp. 68–73.

79 On the concept of a knowledge class, see Peter Berger, 'Ethics and the Present Class Struggle', *Worldview*, Apr. 1978, pp. 6–11. See also Frederic M. Roberts, 'Conversations Among Liturgists', *Liturgy Digest* 2:2 (1995), pp. 36–124.

80 For a moderately sympathetic review of Gamber's book by a mainstream liturgical scholar, see Graham W. Woolfenden, 'The Problems of Liturgical Change: A Review Article', *Eastern Churches Journal* 2 (1995), pp. 185–92.

81 See n. 41 above regarding the 1994 Roman Instruction on 'Inculturation and the Roman Liturgy'.

82 See M. Francis Mannion, 'Liturgy and the Present Crisis of Culture', *Worship* 62 (1988), pp. 98–123 (a slightly edited version of this essay appeared in Eleanor Bernstein (ed.), *Liturgy and Spirituality in Context: Perspectives on Prayer and Culture* (Collegeville, MN: Liturgical Press, 1990),

pp. 1–26); 'Worship in an Age of Subjectivism', *Liturgy 80* 20 (July, 1989), pp. 2–5; 'Worship and the Public Church', *Liturgy 80* 20 (October, 1989), pp. 11–14; 'Cultural Fragmentation and Christian Worship', *Liturgy 90* 21 (February/March, 1990), pp. 4–7.

83   See Frank C. Senn, '"Worship Alive": An Analysis and Critique of "Alternative Worship Services"', *Worship* 69 (1995), pp. 194–224, for a critique of what he calls 'effervescent practices' in present-day North American Roman Catholic and Protestant worship. The problems of tension between culture and Church in Western Christianity are not limited to Roman Catholicism. For Anglican commentary, see Bryan Spinks, 'Liturgy and Culture: Is Modern Western Liturgical Revision a Case of Not Seeing the Wood for the Trees?', in Bradshaw and Spinks (eds.), *Liturgy in Dialogue: Essays in Memory of Ronald Jasper*, pp. 28–49 (see n. 65 above); W. Jardine Grisbooke, 'Liturgical Reform and Liturgical Renewal', *Studia Liturgica* 21 (1991), pp. 136–54; Barry Spurr, *The Word in the Desert: Anglican and Roman Catholic Reactions to Liturgical Reform* (Cambridge: Lutterworth Press, 1995).

84   Aidan Kavanagh, 'Liturgical Inculturation: Looking to the Future', *Studia Liturgica* 20 (1990), esp. pp. 102–03. See also Anthony Archer, *The Two Catholic Churches: A Study in Oppression* (London: SCM Press, 1986).

85   See M. Francis Mannion, 'The Roman Liturgy and Cultural Adaptation', *Liturgy OCSO* 24:3 (1990), pp. 12–26; 'Liturgy and Culture', in Fink (ed.), *The New Dictionary of Sacramental Worship*, pp. 307–13; '[Liturgy and Culture:] A Variety of Approaches', *Liturgy 80* 20 (April, 1989), pp. 4–6. More generally, see Francis E. George, *Inculturation and Ecclesial Communion: Culture and Church in the Teaching of Pope John Paul II* (Rome: Urbaniana University Press, 1990); Matthew L. Lamb, 'Inculturation and Western Culture: The Dialogical Experience between Gospel and Culture', *Communio* 21 (1994), pp. 124–44; Geoffrey Wainwright, 'Christian Worship and Western Culture', *Studia Liturgica* 12 (1977), pp. 20–33.

2

The Spirit or the Letter? Vatican II and Liturgical Reform

MARK DREW

If I have been asked to continue and broaden the discussion which Mgr Mannion has initiated, this is not because of any specialist liturgical competence on my part, for I can claim none, but rather, I must suppose, because my own history has been concerned for a long time with the 'liturgical question'.

Dissatisfaction with the liturgical *status quo*, as well as a conviction that the liturgy is at the centre of all the other current debates in the Church concerning doctrine and pastoral strategy, led me to abandon training for the priesthood for an English diocese in the early 1980s. Dissatisfaction with what seemed to me a too intransigently 'restorationist' agenda led me a decade later to leave one of the seminaries opened in the wake of the *motu proprio Ecclesia Dei* for those who remained attached to the old liturgy, but did not want to follow Archbishop Lefebvre into schism. The Roman blessing for such initiatives brought euphoria from those of us who thought that the traditionalist movement, hitherto marginalised, might henceforth play a constructive role in the crisis in the Church. Subsequent experience led me to a less sanguine outlook. Finally, my experience as a priest in a rural French diocese has led me to reflect long and hard on the current situation of the reformed liturgy, a reflection stimulated by experience of both

the best and the worst examples of the results of the reform
in that country which played so prominent a role in the pre-
conciliar liturgical movement.

The position I shall outline here aspires to be a conciliatory
one, which would encourage those seeking to 'recatholicise the
reform', like Mgr Mannion, those who want a 'reform of the
reform', and indeed those who wish to restore the pre-reformed
liturgy, to see their efforts as complementary and in no sense
opposed. Each approach, I will maintain, may have an important role to play, while needing to be nuanced by a more positive
and realistic assessment of the others as contributions to a
solution of the liturgical crisis.

Perhaps, before going any further, I should attempt to justify
my use of the word 'crisis'. Responses to criticism of the state of
the liturgy, from both Church authorities and liturgical experts,
have long insisted that the application of the reform has been
an unqualified success, apart from rare and temporary local
aberrations. Recently, however, there have been signs of recognition from authoritative voices that there is indeed a crisis.
Thus the Belgian primate, Cardinal Daneels, not usually
considered theologically backward-looking, wrote recently in his
diocesan newsletter:

> In the past Canon Law and the rubrics dominated everything:
> priests conformed to their prescriptions with an obedience which
> was sometimes puerile, for want of being enlightened. Today, the
> reverse is the case: it is the liturgy which must obey us and be
> adapted to our concerns, to the extent of becoming more like a
> political meeting or a 'happening'. 'We are going to celebrate our
> own life experience!'[1]

While the extent of the crisis is not the same everywhere, most
of us will have experience of it in one form of another. I have
already said that in France one finds the best as well as the worst
of what the new liturgy has to offer, but it must be added that
the best is generally found in monasteries, and that parish life
in general illustrates the worst. Truncated and mutilated
celebrations, rites and texts subjected to unauthorised and inept
'adaptation', liturgical song of execrable taste and unashamedly
secular content, often indeed expressing heterodox notions,[2]

all conspire to bear out what Louis Bouyer said in the 1970s: that in the Catholic Church at present there is little which merits the name of 'liturgy'. In the last two decades the progress at parish level has been negligible – where, that is, things have not got worse. Deprived of the sacred, sometimes without even knowing what it is they instinctively miss, many abandon religious practice. A whole generation of young people is growing up believing that the essential purpose of the liturgy is didactic; they get bored quickly and stay away.

How has this situation come about? What has become of the high hopes of the architects of liturgical reform: revitalisation of Church life; a flowering of lay piety brought about by renewed contact with the biblical and patristic roots of the liturgy?

One might of course seek the answers to these questions in factors outside the liturgy itself. The cultural climate of the 1960s and 1970s may be seen, with hindsight, as having been conducive to the 'hijacking' of the reform by those whose agenda was secularising and politicising. This climate has certainly been decisive in encouraging congregations to celebrate themselves, their own cultural and religious identity, rather than the objective historical realisation of an essentially supernatural salvation in Christ. At least in France, the intellectual hegemony enjoyed by Marxism in the post-war period played a capital role: beauty was stigmatised as elitist and bourgeois, the sense of the sacred as obscurantist. Salvation had to be thought of in social and economic terms. In the properly theological arena many French clergy accepted uncritically the thought of liberal Protestants, notably the idea popularised by the anti-liberal Karl Barth that faith must be purified of contamination from 'religion', the latter seen as hopelessly compromised with an essentially pagan sacralising urge in main, inimical to the true Christian worship 'in spirit and in truth'.

In France there has been in recent years a reaction to this trend, especially among younger clergy and seminarians hungry for the spiritual. This is a hopeful sign, but in my view not yet of sufficient depth and clarity of vision. Seminary training inculcates a suspicion of anything resembling an attachment to the past. Gregorian chant is tolerated only on CD, incense and tasteful vestments abhorred. Too often the liturgical practice of the younger generation resembles what one might call the 'fossilisation' of the new rites (the reader will remember the reformers' descriptions of the unreformed rites as 'fossilised'). This means in practice a rubrically correct but minimalist and uninspired celebration, whose musical and artistic expressions seem locked in a 1970s time warp.

But to return to my question 'why?', it does not seem to me that all the blame for the current *débâcle* can be laid at the door of extraneous cultural factors. I would contend that the liturgical reformers themselves, the revised rites and texts they elaborated, and the authority which promulgated the reform – that is to say the Holy See itself – must take some share of the blame. This is because the reforms themselves were too hastily conceived and implemented, and most of all because they went far beyond what the Council itself had mandated. An entire generation saw the entire edifice of the liturgical tradition of the Latin Rite, formerly regarded as sacrosanct, demolished in the space of less than ten years. It is hardly surprising if this generation of Catholics has absorbed the message that the Church today has, with official sanction, turned its back decisively on the past; that tradition has nothing to offer. It should surprise nobody, given the centrality of the liturgy in Catholic life and thought, that this revolutionary attitude has overflowed the domain of liturgy to infect every aspect of Church discipline and doctrine.

This will seem to some a daring judgement, and it will not go unchallenged. The architects of liturgical reform have defended themselves vigorously against the charge of innovation. It is certainly true that many of the more virulent attacks on the new rite of Mass lack balance and scholarly depth. A typical example of these, and possibly the most influential, is the *Breve Esame Critico del Novus Ordo Missae*, published in June 1969 with the signatures of the curial Cardinals Ottaviani and Bacci. Its real author was in fact the French Dominican theologian Fr Guérard des Lauriers, since deceased out of communion with the Catholic Church, having received schismatic episcopal consecration. Although a brilliant representative of the neo-Thomistic school, Fr Guérard des Lauriers was not a liturgist, and may be criticised as having a narrowly ahistorical theological approach. The central thrust of his argument – destined to become the *leitmotif* of traditionalist critiques of the new Mass – was that the new Missal has Protestantised the notion of the Mass by systematically suppressing or toning down references to the Mass as a sacrifice, and by reducing expressions of reverence and adoration towards the Blessed Sacrament. I think these criticisms lack balance and historical sense. In the *Breve Esame* one is surprised to find almost as much significance attached to the suppression of certain genuflections or signs of the Cross as to substantial textual changes, and subsequent polemical writings exacerbated this tendency.

In reality, the motivations of the liturgical reformers were not to Protestantise the Mass. They were scholars who wished to bring out into the light of day the riches of a patristic liturgy which they had discovered with excitement in their libraries. In their enthusiasm, they wished to share their discoveries with ordinary Catholics. They were certainly aware that by adopting texts whose vocabulary was patristic they would further the cause of ecumenism, since this language would be more acceptable than that of the Middle Ages and of the scholastics to those Protestants whose own eucharistic theology was in many cases being 'recatholicised' by the revival of patristic and biblical studies, bringing new insights and bypassing old controversies. If one were to criticise the reformers, then, it might perhaps be because they did not imagine how the abandonment of some modes of expression inherited from the period of the flowering of eucharistic piety in the Middle Ages might cause confusion and scandal among some Catholics, perhaps less theologically sophisticated than they.

This desire to make available to a wider public the riches of a wider tradition, fruit of the theological *ressourcement* which both preceded the Council and gained momentum from it, was one of the factors which contributed to the elaboration of the Council's document on the liturgy, *Sacrosanctum Concilium*. It was perhaps most characteristic of the French liturgists' contribution to the liturgical movement. Another, parallel strand, identified with the Germans, the other strongly represented national group, was the desire – also pastorally motivated – to find liturgical forms less culturally remote from modern man

than the existing liturgy was thought to be. The main features
of the conciliar document are well known; the existing Roman
Rite was to be reformed and simplified by the elimination of
useless repetition and of historical accretions rendered obsolete
by changed religious mentalities. The active participation of the
faithful in the liturgical acts was to be promoted, and to further
this the vernacular languages might be permitted for parts of
the rites, especially those more closely concerning the people.
A wider variety of texts was to be provided, for example by
increasing the number of prefaces, and a new lectionary was to
be elaborated so that a richer selection from Scripture might be
made available for the instruction of the faithful. The Calendar
was also to be reformed so as to be made simpler, and to include
in the Sanctoral a more broadly based and relevant selection of
saints, while removing those who had little living cultus or whose
existence was doubtful.

How many of the Council fathers could have imagined that
the result of their deliberations would be the liturgy as we now
have it? The virtual abandonment of Latin contradicts the will
of the Council and the letter of the post-conciliar texts. Petitions
from local hierarchies soon obtained the widening of the
limited permission for the use of the vernacular to the whole of
the Mass. What began as a permission became in practice an
obligation in many places. Perhaps one day the objective history
will be written which will enable us to understand fully the
part of the Congregation for Divine Worship in this *débâcle*,
amid the confusion of conflicting signals. As it is, the memoirs
of its then secretary, Archbishop Bugnini, show a characteristic
partiality.

In fact, the changed rite of Mass which emerged from the
often heated debates of the Concilium charged with the
implementation of the conciliar decree went far beyond what
the innocent observer at the Council (or the innocent partici-
pant in the votes!) could have imagined, and far beyond the
question of language. An example is the provision of new
Eucharistic Prayers to supplement the Roman Canon (which
some members of the Concilium wished to suppress altogether).
To the three new Eucharistic Prayers first authorised was added
a plethora of unauthorised experimental texts. The personal

intervention of Mgr Bugnini ensured that Eucharistic Prayers
for reconciliation were officially adopted, thus opening the door
to the principle of special texts for special groups. Since then
Prayers for children and for large assemblies have been added.
Might one not wonder whether the very principle of Eucharistic
Prayers for special groups is a factor tending to the dissolution
of the sense of the liturgy as an act of the whole Church,
manifesting its unity and universality?

The outbreak of liturgical anarchy which came in the wake
of the ongoing liturgical reform in the late 1960s astonished
many. It began well before the promulgation of the new Missal,
and was indeed encouraged by official toleration of liturgical
experimentation, in religious communities for example, while
the Concilium was pursuing its work. Bugnini and others
thought that the official promulgation of the revised rites would
put an end to such experimentation. It did not. Twenty-six years
later it still has not. The fundamental perception of the liturgy
for the average practising Catholic has undergone a radical
change. The liturgy is seen more and more as the self-expression
of a Church conceived of more as a human assembly than as a
mystical, heaven-sent and ultimately transcendent reality.
Congregations seem more interested in celebrating their
collective identity and subjective religious experience than the
Redemption accomplished by Christ on the Cross.

There seems to have been a movement away from a
Christocentric liturgy to an ecclesiocentric liturgy, and from a
(badly understood) ecclesiocentrism to a brash anthropo-
centrism. I am often struck by the banishment of the Cross from
the very vicinity of the altar. Most Protestants will today express
a eucharistic theology more consonant with Tradition than that
taken for granted by many Catholics, for the Protestant sees the
Eucharist at least as a memorial of Calvary even if he shies
away from the full implications of this biblical term, while
much contemporary eucharistic practice and preaching
among Catholics seems devoid of any reference to the Cross.
The *ekklesia* seems to be understood less as the people 'called
out' of sinful humanity and won by Christ at the price of his
blood, than as a community gathered together by a common
adherence to (humanistically interpreted) 'Gospel values'.

This is the state of affairs deplored by Cardinal Daneels, in the article I quoted earlier. Again, why has it happened? Doubtless, as has been stated, intellectual and cultural factors extraneous to the liturgy have played a large part. Doubtless, also, if the revised liturgical rites had been implemented in a uniformly obedient manner, the damage to the faith and piety of the faithful and to the unity of the Church would have been vastly less. But can one entirely acquit the advocates of 'official reform', and their work, of having sown the seeds of this situation?

Many apologists for the reform have objected that, in promulgating it, Pope Paul VI was merely continuing the work of his predecessors, many of whom had carried out liturgical reforms. Just as Pius V had carried out the wishes of the Council of Trent in revising the Missal, Paul VI did so at the behest of Vatican II. This argument seems to me to employ a breathtaking sleight of hand. Former popes carried out piece-meal changes which went no further than the addition of new propers, for example, or minor adjustments of detail. The Missal promulgated by Pius V in 1570 hardly differed, as regards the Ordinary of the Mass, from those of the immediate pre-Tridentine period, and was itself almost identical in this regard to that used on the eve of the Second Vatican Council. Pius X, often cited as a liturgical reformer, did, it is true, carry out a fairly radical reform of the Breviary. But it is the Mass which forms the heart of Catholic worship, and there he did little more than revise the musical notation. No Pope, prior to Paul VI, ever went to far as to undertake a major overhaul of the rite of Mass *from first principles.*

If we look at the major distinguishing marks of the ancient Roman Liturgy – the unique status of the Roman Canon, the liturgical year as laid down in the Calendar, the series of propers very largely inherited from the patristic era – all of these have been modified so radically that it is difficult not to conclude, with Mgr Klaus Gamber, that the Missal of 1969 gives us, not the reform of the existing rite decreed by Vatican II, but an entirely new rite.[3] His opinion is echoed by no less an authoritative advocate of the reform than Joseph Gélineau, SJ, who states quite clearly that 'the Roman Rite as we knew it no longer exists; it has been destroyed'.[4]

Of course, the 'destruction' only affects the rites and not the transcendent realities they convey. The essential structure of the Mass, including everything that is of divine institution, is left untouched. Given the guarantee of indefectibility given to the Church by Christ, it could hardly be otherwise. None the less, for Catholics, traditions have always been venerated as expressions of, and witnesses to, the great Tradition: the Deposit of Faith. Continuity must be the rule for all evolution, just as some evolution is necessary if Tradition is to remain living. Now, the only sense in which it may be said without qualification that the new liturgy is in strict continuity with the old is in the juridical sense. The new rite is promulgated by the same authority that codified the old. It is the Roman Liturgy because it is imposed by the Roman Church. In any other sense, the continuity is less clear.

Let us take just two examples: the Lectionary and the Calendar. Before the Council, the Missal offered but a sparse selection of biblical readings. Each Sunday and feast offered two lessons: one generally termed Epistle (though it might come from another literary genre) plus a Gospel reading. The Old Testament was under-represented. On weekdays, for ferial Masses the Sunday readings were repeated, the propers for saints' days often involved wearisome repetition from the Commons (of martyrs, of virgins, etc.), and a small selection of votive masses completed the options. One readily understands and welcomes the Council's directive that the faithful be offered a richer selection from the Word of God to nourish their piety. Before 1969, both German and French bishops had published a yearly cycle of readings for weekday masses. This, plus the provision of additional mainly Old Testament texts for optional use on Sundays, might have been thought to respond amply to the need highlighted by the Council. Instead, the new Lectionary gives us a three-year cycle of three readings for Sundays, and a biennial cycle of two readings for weekdays. One might argue that this in itself weakens the idea of a liturgical year as such, which after all involves the yearly repetition of texts which thus become associated with a given Sunday or feast. Also, the original cycle of Sunday readings, often dating back to the time of St Gregory the Great, has been disrupted. It is by no means clear that the average lay person has the knowledge to appreciate, or even the average priest the learning to expound, a variety of texts whose abundance can seem confusing. To make matters worse, the criteria of selection often seem more exegetical than liturgical. The principle of *lectio continua* for the New Testament reading and the Gospel, crossed with a thematic selection of Old Testament texts to fit the Gospel reading, is confusing, and sometimes leads to tenuous homiletic acrobatics by preachers trying to link up all three readings. To this we may add a disturbing tendency to 'censor' texts judged too harsh for sensitive contemporary ears. Irritating in the Liturgy of the Hours, this becomes subversive in the Lectionary. On the feast of Corpus Christi, for instance, St Paul's warning about unworthy Communion is omitted from the reading of the 1 Corinthians passage on the Eucharist, and this at a time when pastoral experience suggests it is highly relevant!

As for the new Calendar, while it represents an admirable feat of draughtsmanship, it may be criticised for being constructed on entirely abstract criteria. Was it necessary to suppress entire liturgical seasons (Epiphany, Septuagesima, the octave of Pentecost)? As for the Sanctoral, it seems to ignore the essentially popular character of the cultus of the saints, rooted in memories of time and place. Saints' days are shifted for reasons doubtless worthy in themselves (e.g. to clear as many celebrations as possible out of Lent and Advent) but at the price of ignoring these traditional associations in a way which cannot have failed to contribute to the decline in the veneration of the saints. The selection of saints was indeed given a broader geographical base and more modern saints included, often at the expense of ancient martyrs, but the criteria for inclusion seem erratic. In fact the original idea of an extremely draconian reduction in the number of celebrations in the universal Calendar, to be supplemented freely by local churches, seems to have been subverted by the vociferous lobbying of various interest groups for the inclusion of their particular saint. Cynics might spot that there is still a certain preponderance of Italians among those who 'made it'.

But if we are to seek a reason for a liturgical state of affairs in the Latin Church which no less a figure than Cardinal Ratzinger describes as 'globally negative', we have to look further than academic theological or liturgical criteria. We should ask what liturgy is; what its role is in cultural and anthropological terms. What role do rites play in human societies (for grace, in this domain as in others, will not abolish nature, but elevate and perfect it)? Mgr Gamber writes of the liturgy as a *Heimat*, a word we may inadequately translate as 'homeland'. People feel at home in the liturgy with which they grew up. When it is destroyed brutally in the space of a few years, this cannot fail to produce upheaval in their religious life. The abstract reasonings invoked by the experts are beyond them. They will suppose that their religion is undergoing a revolutionary change. Some few will welcome this with enthusiasm; a few likewise will resist stubbornly and cling to the old ways. Most will accept the new *status quo* slowly and grudgingly at first, then more easily as they forget the past. What is lost is the sense of a common homeland uniting each with his neighbour in the pew, and beyond, with peoples of diverse cultures and outlooks. And since what was once considered timeless has been proved ephemeral, there is a loosening of that loyalty which binds a man to his faith, and many drift away into indifference. This is what seems to have happened at the Protestant Reformation, at least in England, and does it not resemble what has happened to the Catholic Church these last thirty years? Has our common liturgical 'homeland', once seen as a concrete expression of the stability of the Church in the Faith once delivered to the saints, been lost forever? It can certainly not be reconstructed as if nothing had happened. But can a new 'homeland' be constructed, preserving as much as possible of what is timeless in the old, incorporating what proves of lasting value in the new?

If we think the answer is 'yes', if we wish to consider how to bring about the construction of a new liturgical *Heimat*, we need to bear in mind that what has been lost in so short a time cannot, unfortunately, be rebuilt so quickly or so easily. All we can hope to do is to help lay the foundations on which future generations may build. Among those who agree on this aim, there remains disagreement about the means, as well as the precise form of the solution to the liturgical problem. Hence the different agendas which Mgr Mannion has schematised so ably and, I think, so fairly. I certainly favour personally the movement seeking a 'reform of the reform', yet I must state that I think that this approach is complementary and in no sense opposed to Mgr Mannion's aim of 'recatholicising' the existing new rites.

Indeed, strategically speaking, that agenda is certainly the most important in the present situation, since it is capable of reaching a far wider selection of Catholics, those who have become accustomed to the new rites and would not feel at home with the old. It would be psychologically impossible, and indeed unjust, to force upon these an upheaval comparable to what we have described. This, however, does not mean it is impossible to imagine that elements from the older liturgy might be re-introduced over time, accompanied by a catechesis aiming to show how these are putting Catholics back in touch with their own heritage and identity.

At the same time, the continued existence of the un-reformed rites, albeit in a form which may appear 'fossilised' to many, will surely prove invaluable in the search for a new equilibrium. The permission of the old liturgy for those who remain attached to it seems to me to be important, not merely to spare the feelings of a minority which deplores its passing, but to present future generations with a living witness to the strengths as well as the weaknesses of the liturgy which inspired so many centuries of Catholic prayer. They will be able to reflect more serenely than we can on what can be reclaimed from a past which has not been entirely effaced. In the meantime those groups which still cling to the old liturgy, though they may be small and often irritating to authority by their stubbornness, show no sign at present of going away. Nor will they, surely, until some satisfying resolution of the current crisis is found in the long term.

There is room for discussion, and indeed frank disagree-ment, about what the precise contours of that solution would be. I would myself favour something resembling the *status quo* arrived at by 1967, a rite having the basic shape of the historic Roman Rite as regards both Ordinary and proper, but shorn of those elements more suited to the *Missa privata* than to a liturgy in which the faithful participate actively. I hope that the use of

Latin and, above all, Gregorian chant will be reclaimed from the oblivion to which superficial fashions have consigned them, without replacing the vernacular, which has such obvious advantages in those parts of the Mass which call for direct comprehension. I would also prefer the exclusive use of the Roman Canon, not because a plurality of eucharistic prayers is in itself inadmissible, but because it is not the tradition of the Roman liturgy to which I think we are right, as Christians of the Latin Rite, to be attached. How much of this may be accomplished one day I do not know, but I fully realise that in the short and medium term the chances are very slight indeed.

So what may we hope for in the nearer future? I think that the short answer is: variety. I have already stated my conviction that the continuing use of the old rite is a key factor. But it seems to me that the current permission, sanctioned by the *motu proprio* of 1988, has two grave flaws. The first is that it leaves it up to individual bishops to accede or not to what the Pope himself calls the 'legitimate desires' of those Catholics who wish to worship according to the old forms; the permission should be general and unrestricted if this desire is indeed legitimate. Secondly, the permission affects only celebrations according to the 1962 edition of the Missal (that is, the last edition before the principles of *Sacrosanctum Concilium* began to be applied). Furthermore, the celebrations must be entirely in Latin, though in practice an exception is made for the Scripture readings. These restrictions are actually the result of an 'unholy alliance' between those immobilist traditionalists who have an 'all or nothing' attitude to reconstructing the pre-conciliar liturgy and those partisans of 'official reform' who fear any 'contamination' of the new forms by older practices. I believe that these restrictions hinder progress. Let me be clear, before going any further, that celebrations integrally in accordance with the 1962 Missal should be available wherever practical for all those who want them. Pastoral sensitivity requires that the 'legitimate desires' of these people be taken into account. The damage and pain caused by the years in which these desires have been refused will take a long time to heal, and require the utmost tact and tolerance from pastors of souls. What I am here suggesting is that those priests who would wish to foster the celebration outside traditionalist circles of a more traditional form of the Roman Rite, yet revised according to the wishes of Vatican II, should be allowed to do so. The average congregation would be hopelessly confused and alienated by a forced return to the unreformed liturgy, but a sensitive use of those options put in place between 1963 and 1967 might bear unexpected fruit. The old liturgy, instead of being confined to a 'ghetto' where it has no practical impact on any but a tiny minority of marginalised Catholics, might then begin to influence the celebrations of a widening group and fecundate their reflections on the future of the liturgy.

There is an element of liturgical practice which I have left until last because I believe it an essential question to be addressed by all those who are serious about reconnecting Catholic liturgy to its traditional sources. Whether we conceive of our goal as the 'recatholicising' of the existing rites or as 'reforming the reform', we ought to address it as a matter of urgency. I am referring to the question of the orientation of the eucharistic celebration. I use the word 'orientation' in its most literal sense, because my point concerns the eastward position of the celebrant at the altar.

If we were to single out one factor which sums up the revolutionary change in the liturgical practice of the Latin Church since the Council, it must surely be this. The word 'revolution' should be taken once again in its most literal sense: the celebrant at Mass has *turned round* to face the assembly. *Sacrosanctum Concilium* nowhere mentions such a change, nor do the post-conciliar texts impose it (although they do authorise it). None the less, it has come to be seen as a binding norm. I have already contended that a whole generation of Catholics has been left with the impression that the Church has turned its back on the past. This receives a very concrete, visible expression in the fact that in most churches (at least in France, where neither Church finances nor the secular authorities which own the older churches permit extensive reordering) the celebrant stands at a table, his back turned to the altar where for centuries the eucharistic Sacrifice was offered. One reason for the change in practice was that the idea became current that it was a return to the practice of the primitive Church. Recent publications have called this forcefully into doubt. Mgr Gamber in his *Zum Herrn hin!*[5] attempts to demonstrate the contrary. His precise conclusions will doubtless be debated for some time to come, but he and others have shown that there is no compelling proof that the president at the Eucharist in the early Church routinely faced the assembly, and many indications that he did not. The early Christians faced eastward, where the rising sun symbolised for them the return of the Risen Lord. The position of the altars in the Roman basilicas, facing into the nave, is precisely so that the celebrant may be thus orientated.

As for the theological justification of the new practice, it is not my intention to cover exhaustively a subject on which much has been written, but to offer a critique of one argument, ostensibly the strongest I think, to justify the celebrant facing the people: it is claimed that his acting *in persona Christi* is thus better expressed. It is above all the Latin Church which stresses the idea of the celebrant as acting *in persona Christi*; the East tends to think of his role rather as being *in persona ecclesiae*. In fact, these two conceptions are complementary rather than contradictory; if we forget entirely one or the other of them we impoverish our theological understanding. Is not the Church, in Augustine's immortal phrase, *totus Christus*, Head and members in mystical union? But if a tendency to emphasise one 'model' (to follow Mgr Mannion in taking the term used by Dulles) at the expense of others often introduces an imbalance into our theology, the same principle may be applied also, surely, to that lived theology which is the liturgy. A given practice may be legitimate in itself, but by displacing others may weaken the capacity of the liturgy to express the mystery at its heart. If the two practices, *versus populum* and *versus Deum*, had been allowed to exist side by side they might have expressed complementary aspects of the mystery. In fact, the virtual monopoly of the former, in my view, distorts our understanding of the nature of the eucharistic assembly. The congregation gives the impression of being a human community turned in on itself, rather than turned together outwards towards the God who is transcendent, the 'wholly other'.

Max Thurian, a theologian not usually suspected of reactionary tendencies, makes the following comment:

> It has often been thought necessary to set up a portable table in front of a splendidly constructed altar under the pretext that the priest must always face the faithful whatever the architectural form of the church. In fact the Eucharistic Prayer itself, which should always be addressed entirely to God, becomes often just another address where the priest, instead of praying, talks yet again to the community.
>
> How often might the use of old churches have permitted the retention of the altar as the place of the liturgical sacrifice and adoration of the Lord: the priest, from the place where he presides the Liturgy of the Word, could address the community while facing it, while for the Eucharistic Prayer until the 'Our Father' he could be at the altar, orientated like the faithful in an attitude of adoration.[6]

In fact, a plurality of positions for the celebrant expresses very well the plurality of manners in which the priest acts *in persona Christi*, even if we choose to remain within that one 'model' as the preferred understanding of the Western Church. For in so far as the priest represents the Lord *vis-à-vis* His Church, he makes Him present as prophet, priest and king. There are moments in the liturgy where the priest represents Christ more properly in His prophetic and kingly roles: when he reads to them the Word of God, exhorts and guides them in the homily, in short when he exerts his pastoral *munus*. One should thus welcome the fact that the priest now faces the people for the first part of the Mass, corresponding to his vocation to teach and guide God's people. Obviously he faces the people when, as Christ their shepherd-king, he distributes to them the food of the pastures of eternal life. But when the priest stands at the altar, he is exercising above all the *munus Sacerdotale*. He stands in the place of Christ, who takes humanity wounded by sin, and offers it in his own person as a pure oblation to the Father. It is surely more appropriate that at this moment he should stand with the people whose representative he is, turned towards the rising sun, which is a sign both of the Resurrection and the Parousia, the *locus* of the final union of man with God. The entire liturgical assembly thus becomes a living icon of the

People of God on its pilgrim march through the desert of the world to the Promised Land of eternal life. The priest represents the new Moses at the head of his people leading them in this new Exodus.

In fact, the whole notion of the liturgy as an icon, as a prefiguration of the heavenly liturgy, although it is mentioned in *Sacrosanctum Concilium*, has not been very much developed in post-conciliar liturgical practice and preaching, where this-worldly concerns have until now tended to predominate. Renewed contact with the Eastern tradition should help nourish reflection on this and other points. A true ecumenism, and a closer attention to the rich traditions of the Catholic Eastern Churches, should do much to provoke a healthy reaction to secularising tendencies in the West.

The key to the way forward I am proposing here is essentially that any possible solution must be a permissive one, and not imposed by authority. My proposal that various forms of the Roman Rite be permitted without restriction will strike many loyal Catholics, used to the rule of law in the Church, as a recipe for anarchy. But do we need a recipe for anarchy? Is not anarchy what we have already? Attempts by authority to stabilise the situation, call to order (sometimes anguished ones), seem to have little impact. In fact the Holy See, by its spectacular climb-down on at least two issues (communion in the hand and girl altar-servers) has undoubtedly succeeded only in weakening further its authority, whatever one may think of these issues in themselves. Dissidents have got the message that persevering disregard for the law wins further concessions. In any case, if what we want is the creation of a liturgical 'homeland' where all Catholics can feel at home because legitimate diversity is recognised, this cannot be imposed, but must emerge gradually by organic growth from various initiatives. The better these initiatives are co-ordinated, the more they follow common principles drawn from the wider Tradition of the Church and not personal preferences alone, the more quickly we can hope to find a satisfying solution emerging as the Catholic liturgy of the future, taking the best of the new and grafting it onto the trunk of the traditional rites.

If we wish here and now to contribute to this solution, we will need to work together in a spirit of tolerance. A more active participation of the assembly in the worship of the Church, a wider knowledge of the Word of God offered to them in their own language, these are without doubt positive results of the reform carried out in the name of Vatican II. But on the way much of our heritage has been lost, contrary to the Council's wishes. We do not know yet precisely how much of this lost heritage, and in what form, can be claimed back. But if our efforts are to bear fruit, we must learn to respect differences of approach and opinion, and to see them as complementary as long as the fundamental motivation is the same – to find a form for the liturgy which will express, as adequately as the inherent imperfection of anything human will permit, the fullness of the Mystery of Faith. Those who remain attached to the old liturgy must no longer be marginalised, or tolerated only grudgingly and with thinly veiled contempt. They in their turn must accept that they have no monopoly on Catholic truth, and that the efforts of those seeking to 'reform the reform', or simply to celebrate the new rites in a manner which makes them more expressive of continuity with the past, are to be welcomed. Adherents of these last two positions must agree to co-operate more closely, not seeing each other as competitors seeking to occupy the same ground, nor stigmatising each other as reactionary dreamers or time-serving compromisers respectively. None has *the* solution. All perhaps have elements of a solution. We must seek it together, recognising that Christ alone as Lord of History holds the key to the future. So the most important part of our common task will be performed on our knees.

Notes

1 'Comment entrons-nous dans la liturgie?', *Pastoralia*, 10 Dec. 1995. Reproduced in *Documentation Catholique* 2132 (18 Feb. 1996), p. 172; my translation.

2 Readers with some knowledge of French may be interested in the following example, approved by the very official Centre National de Pastorale Liturgique and intended for singing during the distribution of Communion:

L'homme qui rompit le pain n'est plus devant nos yeux.
C'est pour nous de prendre sa place,
Pour que rien de lui ne s'efface.

3   For a selection of Gamber's critique of the liturgical reform in English
    translation, see *The Reform of the Roman Liturgy: Its Problems and Background*,
    trans. Klaus Grimm (San Juan Capistrano, CA: Una Voce Press, 1993).

4   Joseph Gélineau, SJ, *Demain la liturgie* (Paris: Le Cerf, 1977), p. 10.

5   Klaus Gamber, *Zum Herrn hin!*, ed. M. Reinecke (Regensburg: Pustet,
    1995), English translation in Gamber, *The Reform of the Roman Liturgy*.

6   Max Thurian, *Le Prêtre configuré au Christ* (Paris: Mame, 1993), p. 77; my
    translation.

3

Whatever Happened to the Liturgical Movement? A View from the East

SERGE KELEHER

Preface

Sacrosanctum Concilium states unequivocally that 'the full and active participation by all the people is the aim to be considered before all else'.[1] Every conceivable device, every trivialisation of the Sacred Mysteries, has been justified in the name of 'active participation'. That being the case, perhaps the most devastating critique of the *novus ordo missæ* is expressed in one sentence by Professor Mark Searle.[2] Professor Searle was among the authors of the 'Notre Dame Study of Catholic Parish Life' in the USA twenty years after Vatican II. This very detailed survey, involving over a thousand parishes, produced the following description of the 'new' Mass in different parts of the country: **'Rarely was there an atmosphere of deeply prayerful involvement.'**[3] Any further criticism of *novus ordo* might even be superfluous. *Participatio actuosa* in the sacred liturgy[4] *means* 'deeply prayerful involvement';[5] any so-called 'active participation' in the liturgy in the absence of deeply prayerful involvement is nonsense and blasphemy.

Characteristics of the Liturgical Movement

The first half of the twentieth century was a time of abundant scholarship on the liturgy, with a strong movement to renew the centrality of the liturgy in the life of the Catholic faithful. Two publications mark the beginning of this movement: St Pius X's *motu proprio Tra le sollecitudini*[6] and Dom Lambert Beauduin's[7] book *La Piété de l'Eglise*.[8] We could profitably discuss some of the particular researchers in the field of liturgiology, such as Anton Baumstark, Bernard Botte, Odo Casel, Yves Congar, Jean Daniélou, Klaus Gamber, Ildephonse Herwegen, Joseph Jungmann, and above all Louis Bouyer. I propose to offer some themes which unite all of them, and which characterise the liturgical movement which they engendered and fostered:

1. A profound spirit of *fidelity to the Church*. These were people who loved the Church[9] above everything except God Himself – and since they found God and loved God *in* the Church, which is the Body of Christ, there is no need to declare such an exception. Particularly in the case of Lambert Beauduin, this love for the Church sometimes demanded great sacrifices.[10] These sacrifices were made with a full heart, and ultimately they bore fruit. One learns from this that there is no authentic liturgical movement apart from the Church – because, in the happy phrase of St Pius X, liturgy is the Church's own piety.[11]

2. An overwhelming *reverence for the liturgy*. One of the very few still-surviving leaders of the liturgical movement from before Vatican II, Father Boniface Luykx, reminds us incessantly that the Liturgy is the 'dwelling-place of God', to be approached with worship and with awe. His own reverent celebration of the Sacred Mysteries, and especially of the Holy Sacrifice of the Mass, gave his students striking proof that he believed what he taught (and his present work as Abbot of Holy Transfiguration Monastery in California continues to give that proof).[12]

3. A dedication to thorough *ressourcement*. The liturgical movement is closely allied to the *patristic revival*, which began in the nineteenth century. The leaders of the liturgical movement knew that one can only understand the liturgy in the context of the Holy Fathers of the Church. Thus they strongly supported the publication of the writings of the Holy Fathers, and the

translation of the works of the Holy Fathers into modern languages. Above all, they taught their students the necessity of reading and studying the writings of the Holy Fathers.

4. A strong desire – even a vocation – to propagate *greater knowledge of the liturgy* among the Catholic faithful at every level. To this end, the liturgical movement promoted the publication of Missals, to enable the faithful to follow the actual words of the Mass as the priest was celebrating. Bilingual Missals for the laity were forbidden until 1897. Desclée published the first *complete* Latin–English missal in 1910; the anonymous editor and translator was Abbot Thomas Bergh, monk of Ramsgate. In the English-speaking world, one must gratefully acknowledge the Summer School of Liturgy organised by Father Michael Mathis, CSC, at the University of Notre Dame, and the series of popular–scholarly books on liturgy published by the University of Notre Dame Press.[13]

5. An effort to make the *Divine Office* – nowadays usually called the 'Liturgy of the Hours' – a much more widely used form of public prayer for the whole Church, instead of simply a priest's prayer book. For this purpose, the better bilingual editions of the Missal for the laity included Vespers, or Compline, or another Hour of the Office, and the liturgical movement encouraged the use of these services in parishes.

6. An appreciation for *authentic liturgical music*, particularly for Gregorian chant,[14] and for the best *iconography* and for the appointments of the Altar and the interior of the Church. Some popular missals included a considerable amount of Gregorian chant, either in authentic Gregorian notation or in modern notation.

7. A profound *interest in the Eastern Churches*,[15] and particularly, of course, in the Eastern Liturgies. The liturgical movement published Eastern liturgical texts, arranged for public celebrations of the Eastern liturgies, and considered that there is much to be learned from the Eastern Christian ways of divine worship. In consequence, both Eastern Catholic and Eastern Orthodox liturgiologists have been closely associated with the Roman Catholic liturgical movement. In recent times, one must remember Mircea Eliade, Archimandrite Lev Gillet, Father Cyril

Korolevsky, Archbishop Alexis van der Mensbrugghe, Father Placid Podipara, Protopresbyter Alexander Schmemann, and many more.

8. A reverence for *Sacred Scripture*, and a support for the development of sound biblical studies, nuanced by an ever-present awareness that the Bible is the Book of the Church, to be read within the Church.[16]

9. A strong *monastic* anchoring. Monasteries have played a crucial role in the liturgical movement: one thinks immediately of Solesmes, Maria-Laach, Mont-César, St-André, Chevetogne and others. In 1995 Pope John Paul II in *Orientale Lumen* wrote very movingly about the indispensable relationship between monasticism and liturgy.

One could sum up all these characteristics in a word which today might seem ironic, but is nonetheless true: the authentic Catholic liturgical movement of the twentieth century is deeply and thoroughly *traditionalist*. The aim of the liturgical movement is to know, to live, and to spread the genuine orthodox Tradition of the Catholic Church.[17] This could easily be demonstrated from the writings and the lives of the leaders of the liturgical movement; no one who is familiar with them would dispute it.

Post-Conciliar Shock

At the Second Vatican Council, the great leaders of the liturgical movement who were still alive believed that they had won the day. *Sacrosanctum Concilium* seemed to accept and endorse their entire programme.[18] Now, thirty years after the Council, one discovers that people who care about the genuine orthodox Tradition of the Catholic Church are in some cases taking refuge in the Eastern Churches,[19] in some cases struggling to maintain the Tridentine Mass and barring the door to anything that even reminds them of *novus ordo*,[20] and in some cases desperately insisting that the problem is not *novus ordo*, but merely the 'abuses' of *novus ordo*, and ignoring the reality that *novus ordo* continues to deteriorate. In the words of the Psalmist:

O God, . . . why does Thine anger smoke against the sheep of Thy
    pasture?
Remember . . . Mount Zion, where Thou hast dwelt.
Direct Thy steps to the endless ruins;
the enemy has destroyed everything in the sanctuary!

Thine enemies shriek where Thine Assemblies used to gather;
they stuck their enemy emblems over the entrance,
emblems we had never seen before.

At the upper entrance they hacked the wooden trellis with axes.
And then all its carved wood they broke down with hatchets and
    hammers.
They set Thy sanctuary on fire;
to the ground they desecrated the dwelling-place of Thy Name.
They said to themselves 'We will utterly subdue them';
they burned down every shrine of God in the country!

We do not see our signs; there is no longer any prophet.
And no one knows how long this will last![21]

What happened? How did the liturgical movement which I
have attempted to describe, and which prepared the way for
Sacrosanctum Concilium (the Constitution on the Sacred Liturgy,
the very first document passed by the Second Vatican Council),
become so diverted that in 1966 Father Louis Bouyer warned
that

> Dom Lambert Beauduin said that the relative fossilization of the
> liturgy in modern times may perhaps have been its salvation. Had
> this not been the case, he explained, what still would have remained
> for us today of the great tradition of the Church? The time of
> mummification has passed, and that is good. But it is not enough to
> change again in order to come alive. We must not permit a Lazarus
> who has just emerged from the grave to be submitted to such a
> decomposition which this time would bring him back to it for good.
> Already we only too often observe how individual aberrations or
> collective day-dreams succeed in spinning a web around the best
> orientations of conciliar authority. For all the defects in the liturgy,
> whether of the past or the present, and for everything that accom-
> panies, sustains or produces them in piety as well as religious
> thought, there can be but one remedy. And this is a return to the

sources, as long as it is authentic and not one that is pretended or miscarried.[22]

Two years later the same author could write that

there is practically no liturgy worthy of the name today in the Catholic Church. Yesterday's liturgy was hardly more than an embalmed cadaver. What people call liturgy today is little more than this same cadaver decomposed.[23]

Father Bouyer continued with the direct accusation that those who purported to apply the directives of Vatican II *deliberately turned their backs* upon everything that Beauduin, Casel, Bouyer himself, and all the others had tried to do.[24] Whoever doubts the truth of this accusation has only to read Father Bouyer's books on liturgy, and then look at the state of the *novus ordo*. Those who have claimed to 'implement' *Sacrosanctum Concilium* have repudiated the foundations of that document, have conceived a different inspiration, and have led the Roman Church in quite another direction from that given by the liturgical movement and ratified by the Council.

Pre-Conciliar Sources of the Crisis

But it is not sufficient to complain of this process. What happened did not happen by accident; the liturgical crisis has roots, and without an examination of those roots there would be little success in any efforts to improve the situation. The following difficulties were discernible in the liturgical situation before Vatican II and have been magnified in *novus ordo*:

1. *Authoritarian clericalism*: the notion that everything must be done purely out of obedience 'because I say so, that's why!' The obedience thus demanded is pure servility; it has nothing to do with interior religious assent, and still less does it have to do with genuine understanding. Thus the parish priest who in 1961 employed abusive language to dismiss those who suggested a greater use of the vernacular in the Mass could and did employ similarly abusive language in 1968 to dismiss anyone who suggested that it would be well to maintain some liturgical Latin and Gregorian chant. The liturgical movement was naïve in

thinking that a Constitution of a General Council would suffice to bring our programme to victory. We should have realised that Vatican II, like *Mediator Dei*,[25] could do no more than encourage the liturgical movement to continue its work.

2. The idolisation of '*practicality*'. This problem is so serious that one can find clear traces of it in the text of *Sacrosanctum Concilium* itself.[26] Father Alexander Schmemann, a Russian Orthodox liturgiologist, was travelling somewhere shortly before Vatican II, and happened to find himself in the company of a Roman Catholic parish priest whom he did not know. Seeking to establish some rapport, Father Alexander mentioned Father Louis Bouyer (who was a close friend). The Roman Catholic parish priest angrily denounced Father Bouyer, calling the liturgical movement a group of romantic dreamers with no concern for the 'practical' life of the parishes. He invited Father Alexander to visit his parish, and for the clinching proof of his liturgical–ecclesiastical worldview said to Father Alexander with great emphasis: 'YOU SHOULD SEE THE PARKING LOT!' Critics of an overly businesslike approach to the Holy Mysteries sometimes suggest that churches are in danger of becoming the sacramental equivalent of petrol stations. Perhaps this parish priest would consider that a compliment.

3. *Uneducated and unconcerned clergy*. Before Vatican II, many seminary rectors and instructors and many religious superiors actively discouraged serious interest in the liturgy; courses on 'liturgy' were little more than courses on memorising rubrics. One of the most damning epithets which could be applied to a student or a young cleric was *amator liturgiarum*. Father Louis Bouyer reports that soon after he joined the Oratory he was bluntly informed that 'You're much too interested in things like Holy Scripture or the liturgy. Real Catholics don't attach such importance to those things.'[27]

Naturally clergy formed in such an atmosphere were unlikely to find their inspiration in the liturgy, or to have much respect for others who esteemed the liturgy at its true worth, as *Sacrosanctum Concilium* was to teach: 'the liturgy is the summit toward which the activity of the Church is directed and also the source from which all her power flows'.[28] Those who drafted the Constitution on the Liturgy were aware of this problem, and thus *Sacrosanctum Concilium* includes several strong paragraphs[29] requiring adequate teaching on the Liturgy in seminaries and religious houses. But in far too many instances these paragraphs were either overlooked completely or abused by those who had a different priority.

This problem, before and after Vatican II, is particularly acute in the case of *bishops*. Shortly after John XXIII became Pope, he pontificated at Solemn Vespers. It was the first time that the Bishop of Rome had pontificated at Solemn Vespers in more than seventy-five years. Not very many bishops seem to have imitated Pope John in this. Francis Cardinal Spellman of New York was an example of the lengths to which the alienation of the bishop from the liturgy could go. Pleading the weight of his other obligations, Cardinal Spellman obtained dispensations from Pius XII, so that the Cardinal never recited the Divine Office and almost never celebrated the Eucharist. He used to attend Mass on Sundays and holy days; on Christmas he would visit an American military base (besides being Archbishop of New York, Spellman was head of the US Roman Catholic Military Ordinariate) and offer a Low Mass for the servicemen.[30]

Cardinal Spellman was an extreme case, but he was not unique. Aware of this serious anomaly, the drafters of *Sacrosanctum Concilium* included these provisions:

> The bishop is to be considered as the High Priest of his flock, from whom the life in Christ of his faithful is in some way derived and upon whom it in some way depends. Therefore all should hold in the greatest esteem the liturgical life of the diocese centered around the bishop, especially in his cathedral church.[31]

However, there is no recognised means of initiating the bishops, and candidates for the episcopate, into the significance and exigencies of hierarchal divine services. Nor is there any reason to believe that an ability to celebrate the divine services well is a major criterion in the process of selecting candidates for the episcopate. Father Bouyer laments the situation, asking rhetorically 'why would it be an "intolerable burden" for Catholic bishops, unless because they start with a false idea of their real obligations, to resume what all Orthodox bishops continue to do as something perfectly natural and expected?'[32] – that is, to conduct solemn hierarchal divine services, both the Eucharist and the Liturgy of the Hours, in the cathedral church on Sundays and feast days. But Orthodox hierarchs, both before and after their consecration, are required to spend a definite period in a monastery and in a cathedral to *learn* how to celebrate the hierarchal divine services.

4. *Irreverence.* I can only report my own experience and my own observation of Roman Catholic liturgy in the United States prior to Vatican II. Two examples:

    (a) *The Holy Table of the Altar.* The rubrics of the Roman Liturgy prior to the Second Vatican Council give precise instructions about the materials, care and position of the Holy Table of the Altar. The Holy Table of the Altar must be made of stone, permanently fixed in place, consecrated by the bishop with relics of the saints,[33] vested on all four sides[34] . . . such altars existed prior to Vatican II, but they were rare exceptions. Usually the altar was a hollow wooden box[35] (and often used for storage purposes, despite the prohibition of this abuse). Is it really surprising that after the Council the 'packing case' became an 'ironing board'?

    (b) *Simultaneous services.* Most people find it difficult to pay attention to two or more activities at the same time. One warm August evening in New York, around 1958, I visited a large midtown church. A Mass was in progress at the main altar. A priest was in the pulpit, addressing the assembly throughout the Mass, although paying little attention to the priest at the altar. A third priest was distributing Holy Communion continuously at the altar rail. A marriage was taking place in a side chapel. Devotions were being held audibly in another side chapel. In the midst of this pious chaos several priests in confessionals were attempting to minister to the penitents. The Blessed Sacrament was enthroned in a monstrance over the main altar. The rubrics of the Roman Liturgy disapproved of the celebration of the

Mass in the presence of the enthroned Blessed Sacrament. Had anyone attempted to point this out to the parish priest, no doubt the priest would have dismissed the complaint contemptuously and invited the complainant to go elsewhere. Had anyone informed the Chancery of the Archdiocese of New York, the complainant would have been patronisingly told to mind his own business, and no action would have been taken. Those who in more recent times object to blatant abuses of *novus ordo*[36] have received exactly the same treatment.

5. An overwhelming *preference for the Low Mass*. In spite of all the protestations to the contrary, the real model upon which *novus ordo* is based is the Low Mass. Low Mass was originally a reduced form of the normal Solemn Liturgy, devised for the use of priests celebrating 'private' Mass without a congregation. However, celebrations of Low Mass in public eventually became common and proliferated; during this inaudible service the faithful would pray quietly in whatever way they chose. Eventually, the custom arose of singing this and that during the Low Mass; the selection of material to be sung did not necessarily have any connection with the Mass.

Gradually, Solemn High Mass came to be perceived as a burdensome form of service to be used, if at all, only on extraordinarily special occasions. Thomas Day, in his delightful book *Why Catholics Can't Sing*, discusses this aversion to the High Mass.[37] Every scholar knew perfectly well that the Solemn High Mass – in fact the Pontifical High Mass – was the 'normative' form of the Roman Liturgy, but everyone's practical experience was the exact opposite: Low Mass was 'normal', and High Mass was a rare aberration for odd people. Ordinary Catholics took great care to avoid the High Mass.

In a certain urban cathedral, there was a Solemn High Mass, sung by a boys' choir, every Sunday during the decade before Vatican II. At exactly the same moment as the Solemn High Mass commenced, a Low Mass began at a side altar only a few metres from the Gospel side of the main altar. The Low Mass was carefully timed to conclude *before* the beginning of the sermon at the Solemn High Mass. As soon as the Low Mass ended, the majority of the faithful left the cathedral! They had 'fulfilled their obligation'; they had 'heard Mass' (though in fact they had not heard a word of the inaudible Mass they had attended). Since Vatican II, there is still a sung Latin Mass in the same cathedral, and a Low Mass still commences at the same hour, but it takes place in a separate chapel – progress of a sort, perhaps.

In Germany, as some ideas of the liturgical movement spread, this preference for the Low Mass developed particular consequences after World War I. Most drastic was the so-called 'dialogue Mass', beginning in academic circles and societies of youth groups, and then spreading to the parishes. This 'dialogue Mass' was a Low Mass, but with the entire congregation reciting all the responses previously recited in a low voice by the acolytes. By the 1950s, the 'dialogue Mass' had spread to the United States, where it rapidly became the mark of supposedly avant-garde liturgical circles. The 'dialogue Mass' soon developed a 'sung' form, but since this was still a Low Mass it did not require (or even permit) the singing of the actual liturgical texts.

The resulting hybrid made the High Mass still more infrequent, and encouraged the spread of a misunderstanding of the congregation's role in the Mass.[38] During this Low Mass, for example, the priest was still reading – in a whisper – the Proper chants,[39] which should all be sung by the assembly. Usually the people did *not* recite the Gloria, the Credo, the Sanctus or the Agnus Dei, which should all be sung by the congregation.[40] Again, the priest read these texts in a whisper. However, the people *did* recite the responses of the acolytes during the Preparation[41] and in particular the *Suscipiat* response to the *Orate, Fratres*. Since the *Orate, Fratres* and its *Suscipiat* response are in origin a dialogue between the main celebrant (presumably a bishop) and the concelebrating presbyters, having nothing directly to do with the assembly,[42] there need be no surprise that making these texts into 'community prayers' without changing the wording has had bizarre results, most notably arising from the mistaken impression that the phrase *meum ac vestrum sacrificium* was a reference to the 'priesthood of the laity'.

This sort of confusion of what liturgical texts belong to whom in the liturgical assembly[43] was to lead directly to such aberrations as the occasional abuse of the entire congregation reciting the Eucharistic Prayer together with the priest[44] and the far more widespread abuse of the entire congregation reciting the *Per Ipsum*[45] together with the priest.[46]

Cardinal Heenan provided a remarkable expression of this point of view in an intervention during the October 1967 Synod of Bishops in Rome. His Eminence said:

> I cannot think that anyone with pastoral experience would have regarded the sung Mass as being of first importance. . . . Our people love the Mass, but it is *Low Mass without psalm-singing and other musical embellishments* to which they are chiefly attached.[47]

Cardinal Heenan could scarcely have been clearer: Low Mass is what matters; psalm singing (let alone the singing of, say, the Gloria or the Sanctus) is nothing but a trivial, objectionable 'musical embellishment' which would drive people away from the Church! It's a pity that Thomas Day missed this particular quote: it goes a long way towards an understanding of 'why Catholics can't sing'.

6. A passion for *uniformity*, and a *terror of pluralism*. The supporters of *novus ordo* frequently extol pluralism and denounce the alleged rigidity of pre-conciliar worship. But if one looks below the surface, a different picture emerges.

Before Vatican II, those who argued in favour of a broader use of vernacular languages in the liturgy met the 'argument from tourism':

> the universal use of Latin bears witness to the unity and the catholicity of the Church. Throughout the world the language and rites of the Mass are identical. No matter where he travels, a Catholic will always feel at home for the Mass he assists at is everywhere the same, not merely in its essentials but in its rites and ceremonies.[48]

The argument is idiotic and rests on several false premises, but it is very powerful emotionally; even people who knew perfectly well that it wasn't true[49] still managed to believe it![50] They wanted it to be true; therefore it must be true. And evidence to the contrary must be kept firmly out of sight. The liturgy should be done in the same way everywhere (in the preparations for Vatican II the American Roman Catholic bishops seriously demanded the suppression of the Eastern Catholic Churches in the USA); nobody should know about the different liturgies of the religious orders;[51] the Mozarabic Liturgy should be locked in its small chapel in Toledo.[52]

Three decades after the Council, the official liturgical books of the *novus ordo* have so many options that one would need a computer to find one's way around. But these options are not all as real as they might seem:

(a) The Sacramentary provides the music for the chanting of the Gospel.[53] In 1981, a Byzantine Catholic priest was concelebrating at a sung Latin Mass in the cathedral of a large archdiocese; the celebrant (and Administrator of the cathedral) invited this priest to proclaim the Gospel, alerting him that it would be in English. The Byzantine Catholic priest went to the ambo and chanted the Gospel. The choir had no difficulty responding. But the celebrant virtually flew across the sanctuary to seize the microphone and announce to the assembly that Father X had sung the Gospel because Father X belongs to the Eastern Church and this is the Eastern custom! It is extremely rare to sing the Gospel at a *novus ordo* Mass.[54]

(b) The Roman Canon, which in a slightly modified form is given as the first of the four Eucharistic Prayers of the *novus ordo* Mass, provides a special variation for the *Communicantes* on Christmas,[55] and the 'General Instruction' of the *novus ordo* missal recommends that the Roman Canon should be used on days when it provides such variations.[56] For many years, it has been my custom to take part in a festive public 'midnight' Mass on Christmas Eve in a large church. Every year, I suggest to the other priests that it would be nice to use the Roman Canon. Every year the other priests agree with me, and lament that we *cannot* use the Roman Canon, *because the text is not in the leaflet missalette.*

(c) The eastward position of the celebrant. Absolutely no official document requires the celebrant to offer the Mass 'facing the people'. The rubrics of the *novus ordo* missal assume that the celebrant is facing east, and require him to turn and face the people to bestow certain blessings.[57] But may God in His infinite mercy be kind to the priest who dares to celebrate the *novus ordo* facing east! One may not even discuss the matter (almost no Catholic bookshops will sell Mgr Klaus Gamber's book on the subject[58]).

On this point, in practice the *novus ordo* is far less pluralist and tolerant than the Tridentine Mass;[59] well before Vatican II it was possible to find places where the Tridentine Mass was celebrated 'facing the people' on a regular basis, and it was not unusual to find this practice done in other places on particular occasions, usually for educational purposes.

What Did We Expect?

This raises a pertinent question: what did the liturgical movement want by way of change, in those halcyon days just before Vatican II? What results were expected? By way of example, consider the matter of language. I personally was a staunch vernacularist,[60] and confidently hoped that celebrations of the Mass in English would be available to those who wanted such a celebration. Two possibilities never crossed my mind, nor do I believe today that any of my elders or my contemporaries ever foresaw these possibilities:

1. We never dreamed that it would occur to anyone to *forbid* the celebration of the Latin Mass! *Sacrosanctum Concilium* makes no such provision; it decrees that the use of the vernacular may be extended[61] but that the use of Latin is to be retained,[62] and that all the faithful should be taught to sing certain parts of the Mass in Latin.[63] We expected vernacular celebrations of the Mass to exist 'side by side', so to speak, with the Latin Mass, which would continue to be considered the normal form of celebration and retain pride of place.

Such an expectation was unrealistic, because most parish clergy were unwilling to maintain anything resembling a choice. In England, the hierarchy tried to legislate a requirement that each parish should offer one Latin Mass on Sundays; it failed. In the United States by 1970, one could not even find a Latin Mass in most dioceses, let alone most parishes.

2. Still less did we realise that 'vernacular' was going to mean a cross between computerese and newspaper jargon. Those of us who were active in the English-speaking countries did not expect the existing Roman Catholic translations to be put into liturgical use; that was not what they were designed for. We expected that *Anglican* translations of the Roman Liturgy, prepared for actual use, would be adopted or adapted for Catholic celebrations. The Anglicans had been using all or part of the Roman Liturgy in English for a long time, and had done a great deal of work on the liturgical chant; why refuse to benefit by this work and instead attempt to reinvent the wheel?

In this instance we were not at fault for our failure to anticipate what happened. The unbearable pseudo-translations of the International Commission on English in the Liturgy are closely connected to a worldview which has nothing in common with the liturgical movement: *secularism*. There have been a number of valuable studies of the work of ICEL.[64] The note which marks the ICEL translations and connects them to the *novus ordo* so intimately is the false but powerful principle of Archbishop Annibale Bugnini that 'the norm for the liturgy and for Church renewal is modern Western man, because he is the perfect man, and the final man, and the everlasting man'. For Bugnini, secularisation was a 'necessary process, something the Church needed to accept and embrace'. Bugnini 'accepted and embraced secularism because he said it was reality, and it was necessary to accept reality. He held to the philosophical view that man is made without God and does not need God'.[65] Such a mindset necessarily excludes anything resembling hieratic or sacral speech. In spite of protestations to the contrary, ICEL does not object to hieratic language because 'it cannot be understood'; ICEL objects to hieratic language because such language is redolent of the sacred. Such language is not horizontal; it leads the worshipper to elevate his heart and soul to the transcendent God.

The Christian East

Just before Vatican II Patriarch Maximos IV of Antioch, who became one of the great figures of the Council,[66] wrote that

> we must not allow the adaptation of the liturgy to become an obsession. The liturgy, like the inspired writings, has a permanent value apart from the circumstances giving rise to it. Before altering a rite we should make sure that a change is strictly necessary. The liturgy has an impersonal character and also has universality in space and time. It is, as it were, timeless and thus enables us to see the divine aspect of eternity. These thoughts will enable us to understand what at first may seem shocking in some of the prayers of the liturgy – feasts that seem no longer appropriate, antiquated gestures, calls to vengeance which reflect a pre-Christian mentality, anguished cries in the darkness of the night, and so on. It is good to feel oneself thus linked with all the ages of mankind. We pray not only with our contemporaries but with men who have lived in all centuries.
>
> We hope that this reminder of the principle of conservation in the liturgy coming from an Eastern patriarch will temper somewhat the ardour of reformers in both East and West.[67]

Did the Eastern Churches have any real influence on the *novus ordo*? For a fairly brief period, the advocates of the *novus ordo* occasionally tried to claim Eastern inspiration, and some Eastern Catholics gave that claim a certain credence. It was a short-lived 'affair of convenience'; supporters of the *novus ordo* wanted anything that would reassure the wavering that the new way was not really such a departure from tradition, and the Eastern Catholics felt flattered to think that despite their small numbers they had influenced the much larger and stronger Roman Church in the revision of the liturgy. The error of that illusion soon became apparent.

These are some specific areas in which this 'Eastern influence' is sometimes asserted:

1. Concelebration. The Byzantine Liturgy in particular permits concelebration whenever the clergy so desire; other

liturgical traditions limit concelebration to particular occasions, if it takes place at all.[68] Before Vatican II, the Roman Liturgy allowed concelebration only at the ordination of presbyters and bishops.[69] Many clergy wanted the possibility of concelebration of the Roman Liturgy to be extended more widely,[70] and *Sacrosanctum Concilium* explicitly directed this.[71] There is no particular reason to believe that the Byzantine example is the motive for this decision, and there is every reason to note that the pattern of concelebration of the *novus ordo* pays little or no attention to the Byzantine model.[72] The Byzantine Liturgy requires each concelebrant to be within the Altar, in full Eucharistic vestments, and does not even foresee the possibility of such an overabundance of concelebrants as would require one or more of the concelebrating presbyters to stand outside the Altar. Our hierarchs, clergy and faithful are shocked by the 'mob concelebrations',[73] to borrow an expression from Father Robert Taft.[74]

2. The administration of Holy Communion under both species to the laity. This is certainly the practice of the Christian East; of that there is no doubt. But there is very little evidence that the restoration of this practice in the *novus ordo* was inspired by the Eastern example. The method by which most of the Eastern Churches administer Holy Communion under both species was rejected from the outset, and within a short time the unfortunate practice of 'communion in the hand' became virtually the norm. This novelty is such a scandal to most Eastern Christians that the Roman Catholic hierarchy in Greece has had to prohibit the practice at celebrations of the *novus ordo* Mass in that country.

3. The celebration of the liturgy in the vernacular. Here, the situation in the Christian East is much more complicated.[75] There is practically no use of liturgical Latin in the Eastern Churches.[76] The original languages of the Eastern liturgies are Greek and Syriac; as it became necessary the liturgies were translated into other languages and modified, in some cases developing into new liturgies (as with the Armenian Church, for example). But in almost every case, the Eastern Liturgies have normally been celebrated either in a hieratic language (Coptic, Ge'ez, Syriac and Church Slavonic) connected to the

history and culture of the people who belong to the specific Church in question, or in a hieratic form of the vernacular language (Greek is the most obvious example). As translations were made into new languages in modern times, the Eastern Churches have generally tried to render the liturgical texts accurately and understandably, but using an idiom which is clearly sacral. Only very recently indeed, in the past two decades, have any Eastern Churches produced liturgical texts in colloquial English, and these efforts are highly controversial and meeting serious resistance. No Eastern Church would tolerate the sort of language produced by ICEL; ICEL's inspiration could not possibly have come from the Christian East.

4. The use of several Eucharistic Prayers. Most of the Eastern liturgies have several Eucharistic Prayers. But even before Vatican II the Roman Liturgy had very broad variety in the Eucharistic Prayer – the 'Preface' is actually a part of the Eucharistic Prayer, and the 1962 Missal gives fifteen proper Prefaces.[77] Elsewhere in the West there is still greater variety: the Mozarabic Liturgy has such an abundance of changeable parts to the Eucharistic Prayer that one could seriously question whether a fixed Mozarabic Eucharistic Prayer can be said to exist at all.

In the provision of three additional Eucharistic Prayers for the *novus ordo*, the Consilium seem to have taken good care *not* to adopt any of the Eucharistic Prayers used in the Christian East; a proposal to include the Anaphora of St Basil the Great was flatly rejected. The second Eucharistic Prayer of the *novus ordo* is alleged to be based loosely on the 'Canon of Hippolytus'; one author[78] alleges that Canon II 'is considered by some scholars to be non-Roman, indeed, non-Western', but does not inform us as to the identity of these scholars. The anaphora of St Hippolytus of Rome is not generally known in the Christian East;[79] its author was a bishop of the Roman Church, and the relationship of the current Canon II with the Hippolytan anaphora is quite distant.

No Eastern liturgy ever devised the composition of distinct Eucharistic Prayers for use when the Divine Liturgy is celebrated for a congregation composed primarily of children!

The Task of the Liturgical Movement

In principle, there must be a 'reform of the reform'.[80] But it would not be well to embark upon that 'reform of the reform' hastily; this would be pastorally unwise and would probably lead to further undesirable consequences. For the immediate moment, I propose a revival of the liturgical movement, based upon the principles outlined above: fidelity to the Church, reverence for the liturgy, study and publication of the Biblical and patristic sources, propagation of greater knowledge of the Church's liturgy among the faithful, the popularisation of the Liturgy of the Hours, an appreciation for authentic liturgical music and iconography, an ongoing monastic dimension[81] and a profound awareness of the theology, liturgy, spirituality and discipline of the Christian East, as Pope John Paul II exhorts us in the Apostolic Letter *Orientale Lumen*. There is no need to start all over again; much essential source material was published, and has continued to be published. Some of the classic works of the masters of the liturgical movement are currently out of print; they should be reprinted and used. The liturgical movement must encourage further scholarship, and regular gatherings of prayer and worship; there is no real liturgical movement without a constant thirst for *holiness*.

I would hope, and ask, that all those interested in a sound liturgical movement might encourage the more frequent availability of the Eastern liturgies, and particularly the Byzantine Liturgy, for the benefit of everyone who desires a more complete understanding of Catholic worship. The *novus ordo* represents a turning away from the Christian East;[82] a greater awareness of the Christian East can be most salutary. Partly because it developed in the uniquely eclectic synthesis of New Rome, which happily assimilated Roman, Greek and Semitic culture into a marvellous harmony, the Byzantine Liturgy is the only Catholic liturgical tradition that is *not* tied to a particular culture.[83] This is the key to the ability of the Byzantine Liturgy to take deep roots in otherwise very diverse cultures; in a time when there is justified concern for the 'inculturation' of the Faith in diverse cultures, the successful Byzantine example deserves attention.

Dom Lambert Beauduin's great principle that one cannot reform what one does not know is even more true at the close of the twentieth century than it was at the beginning. For nearly thirty years, *novus ordo* has had a virtual monopoly in the Western Church. Before there is any 'reform of the reform', there must be some *real* pluralism. The liturgical tradition of the Western Church includes the Mozarabic Liturgy, which for centuries has been confined to a small chapel in Toledo; at least on special occasions it should be available to everyone. An authentic liturgical movement needs a *monastic* involvement, and that in turn requires a renewed use of the liturgies of the religious orders: the Carmelite Rite, the Cistercian Rite, the Dominican Rite, the Premonstratensian Rite, and so on. A 'reform of the reform' cannot succeed until there is a far broader living experience of the so-called 'Tridentine Mass'. For that reason, there should be much greater use of the existing indult permitting the celebration of the Roman Mass according to the 1962 Missal; one cannot possibly understand the liturgical movement and the decree *Sacrosanctum Concilium* without being familiar with that Rite of Mass.

One of the restrictions on the celebration of the Roman Mass according to the 1962 Missal is particularly strange: the Mass may only be celebrated in Latin. This probably does not disturb most of those who struggled to obtain the indult; one would not expect the Latin Mass Society to object to having Mass in Latin! But overwhelming numbers of Catholics are unable to appreciate the Roman Mass in Latin. Without in the least abandoning the celebration of the Mass in Latin – quite the contrary – this form of Mass, like every other Catholic Liturgy, should also be available in vernacular languages, so that Catholics of today and tomorrow may come to know it. 'Vernacular' in this context must certainly not mean the idiom of ICEL. To begin with, there could be an adaptation of *The English Missal*,[84] which has the advantage that suitable liturgical music is available to match its texts. This is not quite an innovation for Catholics; the scant handful of 'Anglican Use' Catholic parishes in the United States are following a liturgy along these lines, using Coverdale's translation of the Roman Canon.

At the same time, there is an urgent need for an acceptable English translation of the liturgical books of the *novus ordo missæ*. The Missal of Pope Paul VI has not yet had a fair trial in the English-speaking world. An accurate, suitable translation into good English could do a great deal. That, of course, raises the question of what standard of English to use. I am not an expert on the English language, nor am I a poet. Perhaps, though, I may suggest two possible alternatives (which are not necessarily mutually exclusive, particularly during a period when the liturgical movement will be working patiently toward the 'reform of the reform'):

1. There could be a translation of the *novus ordo missæ* into the traditional hieratic English of the *Book of Common Prayer* and the King James Bible. Such a translation would be suitable for use throughout the English-speaking world.

2. There could also be *distinct* translations for England, the United States, Australia and other places, taking into account the divergence between (for instance) British English and American English. One of the severe faults of ICEL was the requirement that there should be one 'modern', idiomatic English text for the entire English-speaking world; that requirement accounts for some of the problems with the ICEL texts. There is no convincing reason to think that parallel translations cannot co-exist peacefully and fruitfully. Despite repeated laments over the lack of a 'standard translation' of the Byzantine Liturgy into English, Greek Catholics and Eastern Orthodox are not seriously handicapped by having several translations available and in use.

Restoration of the eastward position of the celebrant at the *novus ordo* Mass[85] would also do much to improve the liturgy. The coercive methods used to introduce the *versus populum* position must not be repeated; the restoration of the eastward position must be accomplished gradually and patiently. But this *is* an attainable goal, and a very worthwhile one.

Likewise the restoration of Gregorian chant, the organisation and encouragement of good choirs[86] and good polyphony, and occasional celebrations of the *novus ordo* Mass in Latin will all be very positive steps.

To avoid misunderstandings, let me state clearly that I am only proposing temporary measures. A successful reform of the reform will not be accomplished in my lifetime. The liturgical movement must set to work patiently, prayerfully, without sparing our own efforts, yet trusting in God *in spe melioris ævi*.

Notes

1   Vatican II, Constitution on the Sacred Liturgy (hereafter SC), Article 14. English translation from Austin Flannery (ed.), *Vatican Council II: The Conciliar and Post-Conciliar Documents* (Dublin: Dominican Publications, 1981), p. 8.

2   Department of Theology, University of Notre Dame.

3   Mark Searle, 'The Notre Dame Study of Catholic Parish Life', *Worship* 60 (1986), p. 319.

4   'This participation should above all be internal, in the sense that by it the faithful join their mind to what they pronounce or hear, and co-operate with heavenly grace': Sacred Congregation of Rites, *Musicam Sacram* (Instruction on Music in the Liturgy), Article 15, 5 Mar. 1967; English translation from Flannery (ed.), *Vatican Council II: The Conciliar and Post-Conciliar Documents*, pp. 80–99; cited passage on p. 84.

5   Joseph Cardinal Ratzinger, *The Feast of Faith: Approaches to a Theology of the Liturgy*, Graham Harrison, trans. (San Francisco, CA: Ignatius Press, 1986), discusses a correct understanding of active participation in the liturgy.

6   22 Nov. 1903; English translation in J. J. Megivern (ed.), *Worship and Liturgy* (Wilmington, IL: 1978), pp. 17–18.

7   Lambert Beauduin (1873–1960) is the 'founding father' of the twentieth-century liturgical movement. On his life and work, cf. Jean-Jacques von Allmen *et al.*, *Veilleur avant l'aurore: Colloque Lambert Beauduin* (Chevetogne, 1978); Louis Bouyer, *Dom Lambert Beauduin, un homme d'Eglise* (Tournai: Casterman, 1964); André Haquin, *Dom Lambert Beauduin et le renouveau liturgique au tournant du XXe siècle* (Paris: J. Duculot, 1969); Olivier Rousseau, 'Dom Lambert Beauduin, apôtre de la liturgie et l'unité chrétienne', *La Maison-Dieu* 40 (1955), pp. 128–32; and Sonya A. Quitsland, *Beauduin: A Prophet Vindicated* (New York: Newman Press, 1973).

8   Dom Lambert Beauduin, *La Piété de l'Eglise* (Louvain: Bureau des Œuvres Liturgiques, 1914); English translation: *Liturgy the Life of the Church*, 2nd edn., trans. Virgil Michel (Collegeville, MN: Liturgical Press, 1929).

9   This love for the Church has brought about a profound connection between the liturgical movement and the deepening of ecclesiology, as may be seen, for example, in Louis Bouyer, *The Church of God, Body of Christ and Temple of the Spirit*, trans. Charles Underhill Quinn (Chicago, IL: Franciscan Herald Press, 1982).

10 The cross marking Lambert Beauduin's grave in the monastery cemetery at Chevetogne reads *vir Dei et Ecclesiæ*.

11 Suitably, Romano Guardini's two books *The Church and the Catholic* and *The Spirit of the Liturgy* were published in English translation (by Ada Lane) in one volume (New York: Sheed & Ward, 1935). On this theme, one must read Louis Bouyer, *Liturgical Piety* (University of Notre Dame Press, 1955).

12 See Peter Galadza, 'Abbot Boniface Luykx as Liturgist', in Andriy M. Chirovsky (ed.), *Following the Star from the East: Essays in Honour of Archimandrite Boniface Luykx* (Ottawa-Chicago-L'viv: Metropolitan Andrey Sheptytsky Institute of Eastern Christian Studies, Saint Paul University, 1992), pp. 31–40.

13 Perhaps we may also voice the frustration and annoyance of two generations of students: some of the books in question offer no indices and no bibliographies.

14 During the 'Beyond the Prosaic' conference, Mary Berry gave an excellent presentation on Gregorian chant and appropriate methods for teaching the chant.

15 For an early example, cf. Dom Lambert Beauduin, 'L'Occident à l'école d'Orient', *Irénikon* 1 (1926); pp. 10–20 and 65–73.

16 There are abundant examples of the fruitful mutual support of biblical studies and the liturgical movement, but two in particular must be mentioned: Louis Bouyer, *The Meaning of Sacred Scripture*, trans. Mary Perkins Ryan (University of Notre Dame Press, 1958; also London: Darton, Longman & Todd, 1960), and Jean Daniélou, *The Bible and the Liturgy* (University of Notre Dame Press, 1956).

17 In writing thus, I have no wish to repudiate or diminish the work of such scholars as Dom Gregory Dix (Anglican) or Rudolf Otto (Lutheran).

18 Louis Bouyer, *The Liturgy Revived: A Doctrinal Commentary on the Conciliar Constitution on the Liturgy* (University of Notre Dame Press, 1964), makes this claim of victory on almost every page.

19 Abbot Boniface Luykx is a prominent example.

20 This is the position of Ecclesia Dei and related groups – although not necessarily of all the members of these groups.

21 Psalm 73:1–9 (LXX).

22 Louis Bouyer, *Eucharistie: théologie et spiritualité de la prière eucharistique* (Paris: Desclée, 1966), cited from the English edition, *Eucharist, Theology and Spirituality of the Eucharistic Prayer*, trans. Charles Underhill Quinn (University of Notre Dame Press, 1968), p. 12 (this book at least has an index, albeit a highly inadequate one).

23 Louis Bouyer, *La Décomposition du Catholicisme* (Paris: Aubier-Montaigne, 1968); cited from the English translation by Charles Underhill Quinn, *The Decomposition of Catholicism* (Chicago, IL: Franciscan Herald Press, 1969), p. 105.

24   Ibid.

25   Pope Pius XII, Encyclical Letter on the Liturgy, 20 Nov. 1947.

26   Article 34, for example, provides that 'The rites should be . . . short, clear, and free from useless repetitions [and] . . . within the people's powers of comprehension'.

27   Bouyer, *The Decomposition of Catholicism*, p. 74.

28   SC, Article 10.

29   SC, Articles 15–19.

30   During the Council debates on *Sacrosanctum Concilium*, Spellman proposed that the Mass should remain entirely in Latin but that the vernacular should be allowed for the Divine Office. This led another Cardinal to remark that apparently Spellman thought the laity understood Latin better than the clergy!

31   SC, Article 41.

32   Bouyer, *The Church of God*, p. 416.

33   Adrian Fortescue, *The Ceremonies of the Roman Rite Described*, 4th edn. revised by J. B. O'Connell (London: Burns Oates & Washbourne, 1932), p. 3.

34   Ibid., pp. 6–7. Naturally if the back of the Holy Table of the Altar is attached to the wall or reredos, the cloths cannot hang from the apsidal side of the *mensa*.

35   Frequently 'marbleised' with paint.

36   Such as the abuses condemned by Pope John Paul II in *Dominicæ Cenæ*, 24 Feb. 1980, and those prohibited by the Sacred Congregation for the Sacraments and Divine Worship in *Inæstimabile Donum*, 3 Apr. 1980; both documents can be found in English translation in Austin Flannery (ed.), *Vatican Council II: More Post-Conciliar Documents* (Dublin: Dominican Publications, 1982), pp. 64–102.

37   Thomas Day, *Why Catholics Can't Sing: The Culture of Catholicism and the Triumph of Bad Taste* (New York: Crossroad, 1991), pp. 40-44.

38   Joseph Jungmann, *The Mass of the Roman Rite: Its Origins and Development*, revised and abridged 1-vol. edn. (New York: Benziger, 1959), pp. 121–24 and 165–67, and Mgr Klaus Gamber, *The Reform of the Roman Liturgy: Its Problems and Background* (San Juan Capistrano, CA: Una Voce Press, 1993), both discuss this sudden rise to prominence of the Low Mass in the 'dialogue Mass' of the 1920s and later.

39   The Introit; the Gradual; the Alleluia, Sequence or Tract; the Offertory; and the Communion.

40   At the 'dialogue Mass' the people did not recite these texts, because the 'dialogue Mass' is based on the Low Mass, and at Low Mass the servers did not recite these texts.

41   The 'Prayers at the Foot of the Altar', as the Preparation is popularly termed.

42 An analogous dialogue is found in the Byzantine Liturgy and in the Syrian Liturgies; it is never recited audibly enough to be heard by the entire assembly. Cf. Robert Taft, *The Great Entrance*, Orientalia Christiana Analecta no. 200 (Rome: Pontifical Oriental Institute, 1975), chap. 7, 'The Dialogue after the Entrance of the Gifts'.

43 This problem was exacerbated in the Roman Rite before Vatican II by the requirement that the celebrating priest recite *all* the texts of the Mass: thus he read the Gospel in a whisper before the deacon sang the Gospel, and so on!

44 This is relatively infrequent, but it has happened often enough that it was necessary for *Inæstimabile Donum* to prohibit the practice (Article 4).

45 The ecphonesis which concludes the Eucharistic Prayer of the Roman Mass.

46 *Inæstimabile Donum* forbids this practice (Article 4), but the prohibition is widely ignored.

47 Our italics. Cardinal Heenan's intervention appears in Scott M. P. Reid (ed.), *A Bitter Trial: Evelyn Waugh and John Carmel Heenan on the Liturgical Changes* (Southampton: St Austin Press, 1996), pp. 68–71; cited passages on pp. 68–69.

48 *The Roman Missal*, revised by J. Rea (London: Burns & Oates, 1961); cited passage on p. 9.

49 Such as the author just quoted, who informs his readers a few pages later that 'in the Latin rite [the host] must be unleavened, but in the Eastern churches leavened bread is used': ibid., p. 44. Clearly the author knew that his previous statement was a falsehood.

50 The ability to know that a proposition is false and nevertheless believe it is a characteristic of fallen man.

51 During the 'Beyond the Prosaic' conference one of the main speakers (in a side conversation) argued that the priests of religious orders with distinctive liturgies should be forbidden to celebrate those liturgies in parish churches, even in parish churches entrusted to the religious orders in question, because the laity would be confused by such diversity. *Plus ça change . . . !*

52 For four hundred years, no Catholic lay person was ever permitted to receive Holy Communion at the Mozarabic Mass which is celebrated every morning in the Mozarabic Chapel of Toledo Cathedral. The restoration of Holy Communion to the laity at the Mozarabic Mass is a welcome change.

53 *The Roman Missal: Official English Texts* (Alcester and Dublin: C. Goodliffe Neale Ltd., 1975), pp. 1007–09.

54 During most of the celebrations of Mass at the 'Beyond the Prosaic' conference, a deacon with an excellent voice chanted the Gospel very well, which added much to the liturgy.

55 *The Roman Missal: Official English Texts*, p. 486.

56 Ibid., p. lxxvi ('General Instruction', Article 322a).

57 Ibid., pp. 386, 401, 510, 512.

58 Mgr Klaus Gamber, *Zum Herrn hin!* (Berching: Synaxis W, 1987); French translation *Tournés vers le Seigneur!* trans. Simone Wallon (Le Barroux: Editions Ste-Madeleine, 1993), which includes a preface by Joseph Cardinal Ratzinger and a postface by Father Louis Bouyer; English translation appears as Part II of Mgr Klaus Gamber, *The Reform of the Roman Liturgy: Its Problems and Background* (San Juan Capistrano, CA: Una Voce Press, 1993), pp. 117–84. Apart from Leoniana – in Rome – I have not found the English edition displayed for sale in any bookshop.

59 The rubrics of the pre-conciliar *Missale Romanum* permitted the celebration of Mass 'facing the people'; the 'Ritus Servandus in Celebratione Missæ', V.3, reads 'Si Altare sit ad Orientem, versus populum, Celebrans versa facie ad populum, non vertit humeros ad Altare, cum dicturus est "Dominus vobiscum", "Orate, fratres", "Ite, missa est", vel daturus benedictionem; sed osculato Altari in medio, ibi expansis et junctis manius, et dat benedictionem'.

60 And I remain so, though I would oppose the *prohibition* of hieratic languages.

61 SC, Article 36, 2; Article 54.

62 SC, Article 36, 1.

63 SC, Article 54; the General Instruction (Article 19) of the missal of Pope Paul VI provides that 'since people frequently come together from different countries, it is desirable that they know how to sing at least some parts of the Ordinary of the Mass in Latin, especially the profession of faith and the Lord's Prayer, set to simple melodies'. In practice one may be morally certain that an absolute majority of Roman Catholics have never in their lives heard, let alone sung, the Latin texts of the acclamation during the Anaphora and the people's doxology which concludes the Lord's Prayer.

64 Two of these studies deserve special mention: Richard Toporoski, 'The Language of Worship', *Communio* 4 (1977), pp. 226–60; and Eamon Duffy's excellent discussion in the present volume of the translations of the Orations. Bryan Morris (ed.), *Ritual Murder* (Manchester: Carcanet Press, 1980), is primarily concerned with the language of Anglican worship, but pays attention to ICEL as well.

65 This description of Archbishop Annibale Bugnini's worldview is taken from an interview with Abbot Boniface Luykx published in *Inside the Vatican*, May 1996, cited passages on p. 19. Abbot Boniface knew Bugnini closely for many years, and considered him a friend. Bugnini was far from unique in holding these ideas; Harvey Cox, *The Secular City*, expresses very similar concepts.

66 Thomas E. Bird, *Patriarch Maximos IV* (University of Notre Dame Press, 1964), gives a brief view of Patriarch Maximos's work during Vatican II.

67   Patriarch Maximos IV, *The Eastern Churches and Catholic Unity* (Herder, 1963), cited passage on p. 226.

68   Cf. Alphonse Raes, 'La Concélébration eucharistique dans les rites orientaux', *La Maison-Dieu* 35 (1953), pp. 24–47.

69   The allocution of Pope Pius XII to the September 1956 Assisi Congress, and a Decree of the Holy Office of 23 May 1957, made it clear that there would be a much wider use of concelebration in the Roman Liturgy.

70   J. McGowan, *Concelebration: Sign of the Unity of the Church* (New York: Herder & Herder, 1964).

71   Articles 57 and 58.

72   Recently the Congregation for the Eastern Churches published an *Istruzione per l'Applicazione delle Prescrizioni Liturgiche del Codice dei Canoni delle Chiese Orientali,* in which Article 57, p. 51 asserts that 'it is notable that the practice [of concelebration] recently established in the Western liturgies was inspired largely by Byzantine usage, interpreted, though, in the light of their own concerns and thus with some different out-comes'. Whatever inspiration might have come from Byzantine usage has been outweighed by other concerns, and the 'different outcomes' are apparent.

73   On watching approximately 700 presbyters concelebrating a Roman Mass in 1976, an Eastern Catholic patriarch remarked in my hearing that 'they go from one extreme to the other!'

74   Robert Taft, 'Ex Oriente Lux? Some Reflections on Eucharistic Concele-bration', in his *Beyond East and West: Problems in Liturgical Understanding* (Washington, DC: Pastoral Press, 1984), pp. 81–99.

75   Cyril Korolevsky, *Living Languages in Catholic Worship: An Historical Inquiry,* trans. Donald Attwater (Westminster, MD: Newman Press, 1957), gives a good survey of the situation in the Eastern Churches before Vatican II.

76   There are a few small exceptions to this rule. Byzantine Churches, both Catholic and Orthodox, like to read the Gospel in many languages (including Latin) on Pascha; a few Russian Orthodox choirs like to sing the Paschal Troparion in Greek and Latin (as well as Church Slavonic) in a baroque setting. In the nineteenth century, some Russian Orthodox hierarchs liked to pray Psalm 79:14 (LXX) in Greek, Latin and Church Slavonic whilst giving the blessing during the Trisagion at the Divine Liturgy; a very few hierarchs continue this practice.

77   Supplements to the 1962 Missal for use in particular countries provide some additional proper Prefaces.

78   Aidan Nichols, *Looking at the Liturgy: A Critical View of its Contemporary Form* (San Francisco, CA: Ignatius Press, 1996), complains (p. 117) of the 'wholesale importation of Oriental-inspired Eucharistic prayers in the *Missale Paulinum*' and alleges (p. 121) that 'the Rite of Paul VI contains more features of Oriental provenance than the Roman rite has ever

known historically (and notably in the new anaphoras . . .)', but Nichols does not provide specific examples of these alleged 'features of Oriental provenance' nor does he substantiate his claim of Oriental inspiration.

79   The only exception of my acquaintance is the Ethiopian Orthodox Church, which includes a version of the Hippolytan Anaphors in a very large collection of Eucharistic Prayers. I have never encountered the Hippolytan Anaphora in actual use in any celebration of any Eastern liturgy.

80   The phrase 'reform of the reform' has come into wide use among conservative critics of the *status quo* of the Roman Liturgy and the ICEL translations of the *novus ordo* liturgical books. I am not at all certain where I first encountered this phrase, but it has been in circulation for about ten years, if not longer. By using the phrase 'reform of the reform', I do not in the least propose to endorse any particular organisation or publication (nor do I know of any organisation or publication using this phrase as a title), and still less do I intend my use of this phrase to support any specific agenda propounded by writers other than myself.

81   Cf. Archimandrite Boniface [Luykx], *Eastern Monasticism and the Future of the Church* (Redwood Valley, CA: Holy Transfiguration Monastery; Stamford, CT: Basileos Press, 1993). Also, Congregation for the Eastern Churches, *Istruzione per l'Applicazione delle Prescrizioni Liturgiche del Codice dei Canoni delle Chiese Orientali*, 6 Jan. 1996, Article 18, states that 'The liturgy . . . continues to be a demanding school which requires an assimilation that is progressive, laborious, and never completely accomplished. Monastic communities are particularly sensitive to this dimension and, therefore, can make an important contribution to the full comprehension and progress of the liturgical heritage.'

82   Mgr Klaus Gamber was a most erudite scholar of the Eastern liturgies; one of his strongest criticisms of the *novus ordo missæ* is its turning away from the Christian East.

83   For a popular exploration of this idea, cf. Archbishop Joseph Raya, *Byzantine Church and Culture* (Allendale, NJ: Alleluia Press, 1992).

84   *The English Missal* (London: W. Knott & Son Ltd., 1958) was originally published before World War I; it is a translation of the *Missale Romanum* into the hieratic English of the *Book of Common Prayer*. Both a large altar edition and a hand edition for the faithful were printed.

85   'The missal assumes that Mass can be celebrated either facing the people or facing the altar': Mgr Peter J. Elliot, *Ceremonies of the Modern Roman Rite* (San Francisco, CA: Ignatius Press, 1995), p. 62.

86   With a music director who knows what he is about, a good choir can do much to *encourage* congregational singing. As Thomas Day reminds us in his books, good music in the liturgy requires serious investment, but that investment brings good returns.

4

Rewriting the Liturgy: The Theological Implications of Translation

EAMON DUFFY

The transformation of the liturgy of the Catholic Church in the wake of the Second Vatican Council was, by any standard, a landmark event. It represented the unfreezing of a liturgical tradition which had seemed to many to be sacrosanct and immemorial, beyond question or change. Almost a century ago the greatest of all English liturgists, Edmund Bishop, could write without a hint of irony that 'With the Missal and Breviary of St Pius V . . . the history of the Roman liturgy may be said to be closed'.[1]

Bishop himself was too good a historian to harbour romantic illusions about the timelessness or changelessness of liturgy. He had a highly developed sense of the historical evolution of worship and in fact he was a strong sympathiser and fellow-traveller with the Modernist movement, and its attempt to demythologise the doctrinaire non-historical orthodoxy of post-Tridentine Catholicism. But neither Bishop nor the two generations of liturgists who laboured after him to reclaim for the present the forgotten riches of the Latin liturgical tradition could have dreamed of the cultural and theological revolution which would come upon the Church in the late 1960s and 1970s, a revolution which swept away not only many of the accretions of medieval and baroque liturgical and paraliturgical practice which they so deplored, but many of their own most treasured convictions about the nature of liturgy and liturgical theology. They hoped that the liturgy, duly cleansed of accretion and distortion, would become, in Joseph Jungmann's words, 'a school of faith'. In the ancient prayers and ceremonies of the Church, Jungmann believed, would be found an endless resource, a great well of wisdom and truth. The Liturgy, as much as or more than the definitions of Popes and Councils, embodied the spirit of Catholicism. It had been, he declared,

> carried along through the centuries. People have scarcely dared to alter it here and there even a little, to enlarge this feature or to modify that symbol. But for us this edifice is all the more precious because we can thus rediscover in the Church's liturgy the deep thoughts and the great prayer of the primitive Church. For us, the forms of expression are preserved which belong to that period when an inspired Christianity faced and defeated ancient heathenism, and in which are contained its ever-effective world-conquering powers. The liturgy gives us a concise picture of the Christian world of faith in strong simple lines. We see a cosmos within which our life can fit into everything which pertains to it.[2]

From this side of the flood of change which has swept over both Church and culture in the years since that was written, Jungmann's vision of liturgical evolution and renewal as involving altering 'here and there . . . a little, to enlarge this feature or to modify that symbol' is charged with irony, and his assumptions about the relationship of the liturgical inheritance to the development of the Church of the present seem naïve and unsophisticated. The liturgy here is imagined as an in-exhaustible resource and a universal panacea. Whatever the question, the liturgy would have the answer, for in its formation amid the first great struggle with heathenism paradigms had been definitively established from which could be recovered Christianity's 'ever-effective world-conquering powers'. From a rightly restored liturgy the Church could renew its youth, and would be enabled to face the challenge of the modern world as it had once faced the challenge of the Roman world.

If there seems now more than a little quaintness and unreality about this, it is mainly because the assumptions it embodies about the classic status of the prayers of the liturgy were quickly to encounter resistance not so much within the Church in particular as within the culture at large, where notions of canonicity and classic status increasingly came and continue to come under challenge. Jungmann's certainty that the wisdom of the ages, distilled into ancient prayers and ceremonies, would equip the Church to confront all the challenges of modern times carried within it a series of unexamined assumptions – about, for example, the primacy and permanently privileged status of a specifically European historical, linguistic and conceptual tradition which went back to ancient Rome. In the era of Vatican II, it would emerge, such assumptions could no longer be made.

Yet without subscribing to all of Jungmann's ideas, we can hardly deny that some sense of the classical and normative status of the ancient prayers of the Church is fundamental to Catholic Christianity. We cannot reinvent Christianity, and for the members of any Church their perception of the nature of Christian reality is mediated through encounter with the tradition. Jungmann's call to attend in humility to the ancient words and symbols of the liturgy, precisely as ancient, was a reminder that real freedom and spontaneity come not from a forgetfulness of who and what one is, but from an immersion in the tradition which enables one to renew and extend it, and so to discover oneself.

A vision much like Jungmann's lay behind the renewal of the liturgy which began under Pius XII, above all the restoration of the Easter Vigil, and it has continued to influence the reforms of the post-conciliar period. But with a difference, for it became clear to those involved in the process of liturgical renewal that a far more drastic restructuring and rethinking of the liturgy would be possible than had ever been dreamed of before the Council, and in that perception the neo-classicising, neo-patristic revivalism of many of the founding fathers of the liturgical movement was swept to one side. The results, as I shall argue, have not been uniformly happy.

Far and away the most momentous element in the post-conciliar transformation of the liturgy, of course, was the universal and unqualified introduction of the vernacular into all parts of the Roman Mass, a development which it is safe to say virtually no one expected or dared hope for before the Council. It was a decision, nevertheless, which was absolutely necessary, and I have no doubt that it was one of the greatest of the transforming blessings which the Council brought. It permitted a level of liturgical participation and comprehension by ordinary Catholics – clergy as well as lay people – which the Church had not experienced since late antiquity, and probably not even then.

That said, however, it seems to me that the actual moment at which the transition to the vernacular occurred could hardly have been less propitious. The post-conciliar transformation of Catholic liturgy, theology and ecclesiology coincided with a period of profound cultural dislocation in the West. Genuine theological renewal became inextricably entangled with a shallow and philistine repudiation of the past which was to have consequences as disastrous in theology as they were in the fine arts, architecture and city planning. Thus the sub-Christian aridities of neo-scholastic seminary textbooks were exchanged for a mess of paperbacks, and pious psycho-babble replaced the smug certainties of the older orthodoxy. There was a widespread and undiscriminating collapse of confidence in Catholic theological tradition, and, as a result, some of the least happy developments within the Churches of the Reformation, and indeed within the secular culture of the 1960s and early 1970s, were eagerly embraced as theologically progressive – signs of the times, stirrings of the Spirit.

The most obvious casualty in all this was a sense of the living reality of tradition. Indeed the concept itself became a flag which was trampled on by those who saw that the Church needed, and needed desperately, to change, but who imagined the Catholic past not as a resource for change, but as a hindrance and a burden. And so the flag was increasingly abandoned to self-styled 'traditionalists', who saw in the notion of tradition a charter for reaction, and who found in an uncritical and blanket loyalty to an undifferentiated (though in fact highly selective) past a corset or a suit of armour, rather than an animating principle.

But while these battle-lines were forming and hardening, the work of transforming and then of Englishing the liturgy was undertaken, and it is to the consequences of that latter process that I want to devote the rest of this chapter. I shall not be concerned here with the liturgical reforms themselves, but with the theological character of the English version of the Roman Missal published in 1973. This unloved and unlovely document is now, happily, approaching the end of its working life, for a revised translation of the whole Sacramentary is currently making its slow way through the machinery of the Episcopal Conferences, and should be in use by the end of the millennium. That revision has been undertaken in part at least out of an acute sense of the shortcomings of the 1973 version. This, therefore, seems an appropriate moment to attempt an assessment of the theological character and impact of the 1973 Missal. The text itself certainly warrants such an exercise, for it has shaped the liturgical sensibilities and experience of a whole generation of Catholics. For English-speaking Catholics under the age of forty-five, it *is* the Roman Liturgy. What I want to do in this chapter is to try to assess the extent to which this English Missal succeeded in conveying what Edmund Bishop called 'the genius of the Roman Rite'. How far was the 1973 book an act of translation and repristination, which made the resources of the Roman Rite available, and how far was it in fact a failure to achieve just that, and instead the provision of an alternative to the Missal? And since we say that *lex orandi, lex credendi*, what version of Christian truth is to be found embedded in the 1973 text?

The obvious place to begin such an enquiry might seem to be with the ancient Roman Canon of the Mass, and indeed essential clues to both the successes and the failures of the 1973 Missal can be gained by a close examination of the translation of the Roman Canon which it contained. If we can form a judgement about the faithfulness or otherwise of the English version of this, the central prayer of every missal for over a millennium, we will have established some pointers for our enquiry as a whole. The version of the Canon of the Mass included as Eucharistic Prayer I in the 1973 Missal was in fact one of the first fruits of the vernacular movement, having been produced in 1967–68, and retained subsequently. It has been singled out for high praise by the ICEL drafters of the new version of the Sacramentary, in the introductory material recently provided to the Bishops' Conferences, as being 'dignified and prayerful', and as having 'captured the formality and solemnity of the Latin text'.[3] I am bound to say that I take a less favourable view of the matter. The 1973 version, and for that matter the forthcoming revision, involved a series of decisions which in fact ensured that the translation departed very markedly from the specific character of the Latin original. Translating the Canon, of course, was no easy task. The Latin text was in many ways an embarrassment to professional liturgists, because it appeared to lack elements which were held to be fundamental to any good eucharistic prayer. It is essentially a long prayer or rather a patched-together series of prayers, of supplication and blessing, and of almost relentlessly insistent offering, with very little in the way of direct 'praise and thanksgiving'. It begins, strikingly but puzzlingly, with a resounding 'YOU, THEREFORE' (a 'therefore' which seemed to worry the liturgists). In addition, it has no epiclesis, it has yards of saints' names, and the intercessions are broken up into two chunks before and after the words of institution. It is characterised by a whole range of rhetorical devices calculated to turn a translator's hair white – lists, repetitions, the piling up of near-synonyms apparently derived from Roman legal terminology.[4]

The invention of Eucharistic Prayers II–IV was designed, as everyone knows, to rectify these 'defects' in the Roman Canon. But in addition, the English version of the Canon tried to tone down these 'faults' in a variety of ways – the lists of synonyms were rationalised, the repetitions eliminated, and the phrase 'We come to you with praise and thanksgiving', which has no warrant in the Latin, was inserted to supply what was felt to be a major theological lacuna. Above all, the distinctive and very prominent humility of address to God which is such a feature of the Roman Canon was systematically removed, and qualifying adverbs and adjectives which increased this deference of address – like 'most merciful', 'holy', 'venerable' and so on – were not translated. So, for example, in the opening lines of the prayer the phrase 'supplices rogamus ac petimus' was rendered, baldly, 'we ask', setting a benchmark for translation practice throughout the rest of the missal. It might of course be argued that here was a simple adjustment of tone for a democratic age, involving no point of theological substance. But the rhetorical humility of the Latin was not in fact a marginal element in the text: it was heavily emphasised in late antiquity and the Middle Ages by the profound inclination of the celebrant and ministers at this point (as it was later at the *Supplices te rogamus*). What appears a minor adjustment because deferential forms don't seem to go too well in everyday English speech was in fact a radical departure from one of the most distinctive features of the Latin liturgical tradition, with real and far-reaching theological implications. The shift in rhetorical pitch reflected shifting perceptions of the nature of our relationship with the God addressed. In fact, it could be said, the translation tried hard to tone down precisely those stylistic aspects of the Roman Canon that might be regarded as most characteristic and idiosyncratic about it.

These features of the translation certainly reflected judgements about what was or was not appropriate in direct address to God – that is, a theological judgement – rather than any intrinsic problem about catching the tone of the original in English. The translators seem to have been opposed to rhetorical repetition, despite the fact that Cranmer had successfully naturalised this aspect of the Roman Canon triumphantly in his prayers: it would have been perfectly possible to reproduce at least some of the effects of the Latin style of the Canon in English. No equivalent, for example, was offered for the adjective 'Clementissime' at the opening of the Canon, despite the venerable liturgical pedigree in English of the phrase 'Most Merciful'. The translators would have done well to borrow here the resounding opening of Cranmer's General Confession, 'Almighty and most merciful Father', which would have captured the solemnity of the Latin.

It would be quite unfair to suggest that the ICEL text had no merits, of course. Indeed, at a number of points, it pulled off what seem to me quite brilliant bravura acts of improvisation. Take a particularly difficult section of the canon, the *Quam Oblationem*:

Quam Oblationem tu, Deus, in omnibus, quaesumus, benedictam, adscriptam, ratam, rationabilem, acceptabilemque facere digneris.

This is a very characteristic example of the rhetorical style of the Latin original, and of the fiendish problems involved in rendering it into meaningful English. Should one aim at reproducing the hypnotic, repetitious effect of the string of very abstract adjectives in the original? And how is one to translate words like 'adscriptam', or even more difficult, 'rationabilem'? Hovering behind the Latin, of course, is Romans 12:1 – 'I beseech you therefore, brethren, by the mercy of God, that you present your bodies, a living sacrifice, holy, pleasing unto God, your reasonable service.'

The solution adopted to these difficulties in the translation was drastic but in some ways very good indeed – 'Bless and approve our offering; make it acceptable to you, an offering in Spirit and in truth'. Now, 'an offering in Spirit and in truth' seems to me a virtuoso rendering of 'rationabilem': but it is not in any straightforward sense direct translation, and indeed it has the effect of switching the theological reference of the whole passage from Romans 12:1 to John 4:24: God is a Spirit, and he that worships him must worship him in Spirit and in truth – in effect it rewrites, rather than translates, the original. One can defend the rewriting in this instance, but it does need to be recognised as such. And of course this solution also deliberately sacrifices the hypnotic mantra quality of the Latin.

The shift of theological reference in that passage seems to me largely successful, *if* one once accepts the validity of the procedure – in effect a creative adaptation of the passage rather than a strict translation. All too often, however, such shifts seemed to involve a mere loss of resonance and theological context, rather than an attempt to find equivalents which made more sense in English. Take, for example, the magnificent lines in the prayer of oblation immediately after the words of institution:

Offerimus praeclarae maiestati tuae de tuis donis ac datis hostiam puram, hostiam sanctam, hostiam immaculatam, panem sanctum vitae aeternae et calicem salutis perpetuae.

Once again, the English version made no attempt to reproduce the solemn repetition in the Latin – 'a pure sacrifice, a holy sacrifice, an unblemished sacrifice', offering instead only 'this holy and perfect sacrifice'. But, rhetorical lowering apart, 'perfect sacrifice' was in fact a very poor rendering of the Latin word 'immaculatum', a phrase surely meant to recall the dozens of times the word 'unblemished' occurs to describe the victims for Old Testament sacrifice, and the coming together in the Vulgate version of Colossians 1:22 of the notion of both a holy and an unblemished sacrifice. The word 'unblemished' was presumably rejected as unfamiliar and archaic, but it was precisely its distinctiveness which would have helped underline the biblical resonances and the theological contextualising of the notion of sacrifice implicit in the original. And one can only speculate as to why no translation whatever was offered for the word 'puram'.

We can see the same theological shrinkage in the next paragraph of the Canon, the *Supra Quae*, with its resonant evocation of the sacrifices of Abel, Abraham and Melchisidech. The tremendous climax of this section – 'sanctum sacrificium, immaculatam hostiam', was totally suppressed, and once again the key word, 'unblemished', was missing.

There is of course a whole debate about appropriate language registers and the danger of an alienating cultural embarrassment in translation which I can't enter into here, but which it wouldn't be unfair to sum up in terms of a 1960s preference for unbleached hessian rather than gold brocade. But the meaning is the message, as another 1960s figure used to like to say, and I hope I have said enough to indicate that changes in rhetorical register of this sort are never merely matters of what colour of paper to wrap the gift in, but do in fact involve significant shifts of meaning.

But in what follows I want to concentrate on the short variable prayers of the propers – what we used to call the Collect, Secret and Post-Communion prayers. Though the post-conciliar liturgy contains many new prayers, most of these short prayers were taken direct or with light revision from the ancient sacramentaries of the Roman Church, and indeed one of the most attractive and notable features of the Missal of Paul VI is the number of these ancient prayers which it restored to currency. Edmund Bishop had characterised the genius of the Roman Rite in two words, sobriety and sense, and these prayers amply embody those virtues. In marked contrast to many of the longer and more discursive prayers of other rites, especially those of the East, these crisp and often tightly structured prayers offer a unique glimpse of Roman tradition at its most profound and most memorable. Fidelity to the tradition would demand faithfulness in transmitting something at least of the quality of these prayers into the vernacular.

In discussing the distinctive theological merits of the Roman liturgy, Cipriano Vagaggini, one of the key figures in the production of the post-conciliar Mass, singled out the notion of a 'sacrum commercium', a holy exchange, in the eucharistic offering, which is so central in the Roman Canon. Bread and wine, he wrote, 'are chosen from among the gifts God has given us and are offered to him as a symbol of the offering of ourselves, of what we possess and of the whole of material creation. In this offering we pray God to accept them, to bless them and to transform them through his Spirit into the Body and Blood of Christ, asking him to give them back to us transformed in such a way that through them we may, in the Spirit, be united to Christ and to one another, sharing in fact in the divine nature'.[5]

Vagaggini was discussing the theological focus of the Roman Canon, but this notion of a 'holy exchange' in fact underlies many of the most characteristic prayers of the Roman Rite, and could even be claimed, I think, as one of its defining features. The 1973 Missal's success or failure in handling this aspect of the Roman tradition will therefore provide a good litmus test for its general theological character.

In the Missal its characteristic form is binary: prayers over the offerings or after Communion repeatedly explore the paradox that earthly and temporal things become, by the power of God, vehicles of eternal life. The Missal never tires of this dialectic, and prayer after prayer rings the changes on it. Here, by way of a representative example, is the prayer after Communion for the eighth Sunday of ordinary time.[6]

Satiati munere salutari tuam, Domine, misericordiam deprecamur, ut, hoc eodem quo nos temporaliter vegetas sacramento, perpetuae vitae participes benignus efficias.

This is a remarkably rich prayer in many ways: here I would just draw your attention to the phrase 'nos temporaliter vegetas'. 'Vegetas' in the Vulgate version of Genesis 9:15 is what souls do to bodies;[7] it is the life force itself, filling inanimate things with motion and growth. So the prayer may be loosely translated.

Having fed full on your saving gift, Lord, we humbly beg your
    mercy:
through this sacrament you make us flourish in this world of time;
through this same sacrament, in your goodness,
make us sharers in the life that has no end.

Here now is what the 1973 Missal makes of this.

God of salvation, may this sacrament which strengthens us here on
    earth bring us to eternal life.

This, I am sure you will agree, is very depressing. Gone is the saving gift, gone the vivid image of diners stuffed full to bursting with good things, gone is the distinctive force of 'vegetas', gone is the contrast and pairing between 'temporaliter' and 'perpetuae'. Moreover, the whole prayer has been Pelagianised. The agent of both the human flourishing and the sharing of eternal life in the original is the Lord himself: 'you make us flourish ... make us sharers'. In the translation, it is 'this sacrament' which will bring us to eternal life. Of course, it is implicit even in the English prayer that God is ultimately responsible for the effect of the sacrament, but it is only implicit, whereas the Latin insists on it. I don't think this is a matter of splitting hairs. As we shall see, this shift towards an emphasis on the primacy of human religious activity or experience, at the expense of the Latin Missal's relentless emphasis on the agency of God, is a striking feature of the 1973 version.

What we have here, then, cannot strictly be called a translation: it is a loose and flaccid paraphrase, which empties out the distinctive content of the original, and which lacks the binary structure which gives the original its force and memorability. Incidentally, one may fairly take the version provided in the new sacramentary as an indicator of its general character. While it omits important nuances from the prayer, in particular its deference of tone and supplicatory character, nevertheless is a vast improvement on 1973, making the essential point. If it takes some liberties, it is nevertheless a real translation:

> Merciful Lord, we have feasted at your banquet of salvation.
> Through this sacrament
> which nourishes our lives on earth,
> make us sharers in eternal life.

Take now another example, the ancient Gregorian prayer over the gifts prescribed for the fourth Sunday of Easter.

> Concede, quaesumus, Domine, semper nos per haec mysteria paschalia gratulari,
> ut continua nostrae reparationis operatio
> perpetuae nobis fiat causa laetitiae.

This is a playful prayer, which takes the idea of the Church's annually repeated celebration of Easter and moves from the fact of the temporal repetition of the feast, through the unending work of grace which that repeated action mediates to us, to the perpetual joy of heaven which will be its fulfilment – note the progression through three types of endlessness, 'semper' 'continua', 'perpetua'. There is also a play here, notice, on the word 'operatio', which can simply mean work, business, performance, but which may also mean specifically a liturgical performance. So a rough translation might run

> Grant, we beseech you, Lord, always to rejoice through these Easter mysteries
> so that the ongoing work/celebration of our renewal
> may be to us the cause of unending joy.

The 1973 version, in its very first line, sabotages the play on repetition and endlessness, by refusing to offer any translation of 'semper'.

> Lord, restore us by these Easter mysteries.
> May the continuing work of our redeemer bring us eternal joy.

Not only has the threefold variation on the idea of recurrence gone, but an ambiguity has been introduced into the prayer. What, exactly, is meant here by 'the continuing work of our redeemer'? It is not securely tied, as the original is, to the annually recurring Easter celebration – to the Easter Mass; the whole prayer has lost its focus and energy.

Finally, a simpler example, the straightforward but excellent prayer over the gifts for the tenth Sunday of ordinary time.

Respice, Domine, quaesumus, nostram propitius servitutem,
ut quod offerimus sit tibi munus acceptum,
et nostrae caritatis augmentum.

This prayer once again plays on the dual character of the liturgical offering, exploring quite simply its Godward and its Churchward dimensions. It may be translated

Look with favour, we beseech you Lord, on the service we render you
so that what we offer may be for you an acceptable gift,
and for us an increase of love.

The 1973 Missal once again sabotages the distinctive energy of the prayer.

Lord, look with love on our service. Accept the gifts we bring and help us grow in Christian love.

There is now no discernible link between the three elements of the prayer, for what we are left with is essentially three disjointed petitions, with the final request for a growth of love in particular completely unconnected by any logic to the two petitions which concern the acceptability of the offering.[8]

So far, I have been focusing on prayers over the gifts or after Communion, prayers which, like the Canon, reflect directly on the meaning of the eucharistic action. I have suggested that the 1973 Missal fairly consistently fails to deliver the essential quality of these prayers, but the examples I have given do not suggest much in the way of a theological consistency about the translations. But I did mention the evident Pelagianising tendency at work in the rendering of my first example, the post-communion prayer *Satiati munere salutari*. This Pelagianising tendency becomes much more striking if we consider the translations of the collects of the Missal. These collects include some of the greatest prayers of the Latin Church, and have the added advantage of having inspired Cranmer to some of his most marvellous feats of translation: time and again the versions of these prayers in the Book of Common Prayer render virtually exactly and fully both the rhetorical force and the theological depth of the Latin originals. Time and again, alas, the 1973 versions subvert both. And here, I do think we can see some of the more facile dimensions of the theological fashions of the 1960s and early 1970s at work.

Let us take as an example the beautiful collect for the eleventh Sunday in ordinary time:

> Deus in te sperantium fortitude, invocationibus nostris adesto propitius,
> et, quia sine te nihil potest mortalis infirmitas,
> gratiae tua praesta semper auxilium,
> ut, in exsequendis mandatis tuis,
> et voluntate tibi et actione placeamus.

This is an archetypical Roman prayer, with its massive insistence on the trustworthiness of God, and the corresponding frailty of human nature, and its paradoxical combination of an insistence on our helplessness without grace, with a call to the service of God in will and in action. Here is Cranmer's version: not quite perfect, perhaps, but near enough.

> O God, the strength of all them that put their trust in thee,
> mercifully accept our prayers;
> and because through the weakness of our mortal nature
> we can do no good thing without thee,
> grant us the help of thy grace,
> that in keeping of thy commandments we may please thee,
> both in will and deed;
> through Jesus Christ our Lord.

And here, by contrast, is the 1973 version.

> Almighty God, our hope and our strength,
> without you we falter.
> Help us to follow Christ and to live according to your will.

The inadequacy and inaccuracy of this translation almost beggars belief, but there is more here than ineptitude. At every point in the prayer the insistence of the original on the impotence for good of unaided human nature, and on the primacy of grace, is weakened or downright contradicted. God is not now 'the strength of them that put their trust in thee', but, much more vaguely, 'our hope and our strength': strength is not seen here as proceeding from hope, but as a parallel quality. The stern insistence of the original that without God 'mortal frailty can do *nothing*' – 'nihil potest mortalis infirmitas' becomes the feeble 'without you we falter'. Grace is no longer even mentioned, the strong phrase 'auxilium gratiae' becoming simply 'help us', while the reference to the following of the commandments is edited out, being replaced by a phrase about 'following Christ' which has no warrant in the original. The insistence of the original that the external following of the commandments, under grace, can become not merely an external obedience, but a means of pleasing God 'both in will and in deed', is thus totally lost, the pairing of our actions and will becoming blurred into an unfocused reference to the will of God. In short, a magnificently balanced Augustinian meditation on the dialectic of grace and obedience becomes a vague and semi-Pelagian petition for help in case we falter.[9]

The same forces can be seen at work in the rendering of the collect for the thirtieth Sunday of ordinary time, another ancient prayer perfectly embodying an Augustinian theology of grace.

> Omnipotens sempiterne Deus,
> da nobis fidei, spei et caritatis augmentum,
> et, ut mereamur assequi quod promittis,
> fac nos amare quod praecipis.

In this prayer the paradoxes of grace are celebrated. Faith, hope and charity are pleaded for as God's gifts, and the notion of our deserving or meriting the promises of God is turned on its head, for this deserving is itself the fruit of God's gift. Once again, outward obedience must be replaced by the movement of the whole heart and will – we must *love* God's commandments to win heaven, but such love will not be our deserving, for God must create that love within us – 'fac nos'. Here then is Cranmer's version.

> Almighty and everlasting God,
> give unto us the increase of faith, hope and charity;
> and, that we may obtain that which thou dost promise,
> make us to love that which thou dost command;
> through Jesus Christ our Lord.

The paradox has been weakened a little here by Cranmer's Protestant discomfort with the notion of deserving or merit – *ut mereamur assequi* becomes simply 'that we may obtain' – but this is in every other way a glorious version, which retains the balance and even much of the rhythm of the original. Here is the 1973 rendering.

> Almighty and ever-living God, strengthen our faith, hope and love.
> May we do with loving hearts what you ask of us
> and come to share the life you promise.

Once again, this moves in the direction of a vague semi-Pelagianism. With a little help from God – strengthening, notice, *our* faith, hope and love, a possessive use of 'our' quite opposite in effect to the Latin's *'da* nobis augmentum' – with that little bit of help, then, we will do with loving hearts not what is commanded, notice, but what is 'asked', and so, naturally, share God's life. Gone is any reference to God's promise, and the whole point of the original, that we can't do what God wants unless he gives us both the desire and the power to love his commandments, is eroded and lost.

I said that I thought one could clearly see behind many of these changes the influence of some of the more facile aspects of the theological ethos of the late 1960s and early 1970s. Even when these tendencies don't go as far in a Pelagian direction as in the examples I've just been considering, they are ubiquitous, and the overall effect is the relaxing of the theological tension which is so creative and exhilarating a feature of the ancient Roman collects. Take the Gregorian prayer which is now the collect for the twelfth Sunday of ordinary time.

Sancti nomini tui, Domine,
timorem pariter et amorem fac nos habere perpetuum,
quia numquam tua gubernatione destituis,
quos in soliditate tuae dilectionis instituis.

This is a wonderful prayer, one of the most carefully balanced of all the collects of the Missal, but for that very reason fiendishly difficult to translate. For once Cranmer's version, for the second Sunday after Trinity in the Book of Common Prayer,[10] though it is very fine in its own right, does not really match the original, so I am thrown back on my own more modest resources. A rough translation might run as follows:

Grant us, Lord, not only a constant fear of your Holy Name,
but also a constant love of it,
for you leave no one without your guidance
whom you have firmly established in your love.

There are several weaknesses in my version: 'Grant us' does not sufficiently convey the starkness of 'fac nos habere' – 'make us to have', with its strong insistence on God's initiative and the overwhelming nature of his grace, which always achieves his ends. In addition, the word 'gubernatio' is far more eloquent in Latin than 'guidance' is in English. The Latin word is primarily associated with the helmsman of a ship, so that a better version might be 'you leave no one rudderless' – the whole image is one of rescue from aimlessness and loss by God's steady hand at the helm, or the contrast between the solid grounding which the love of God gives us and the aimless rise and fall of a ship adrift. Nevertheless, I hope my version brings out some of the excellences of the prayer. As will be evident, it turns on a play between the concepts of love and fear, and behind the prayer there hover a whole host of biblical echoes: Psalm 111:9–10, 'Holy and terrible is his name, the fear of the Lord is the beginning of wisdom'; 1 John 4:16–18, 'God is love, and he who abides in love abides in God . . . there is no fear in love, but perfect love casts out fear'; Ephesians 3:17, 'being rooted and grounded in love', and so on. Notice, it is absolutely essential for the meaning of the prayer that both fear and love should be explicitly played off against each other, for the prayer moves from the fear of God's holy name to the greater and more wonderful reality of the love of that name, that is, of God himself, and to the fact that our salvation, our sense of direction and of being held and guided by God, springs not from fear, appropriate as fear might be before the majesty of his name, but from his saving mercy in establishing us in his love.

With all these points noted, let us turn to the 1973 version.

> Father, guide and protector of your people,
> grant us an unfailing respect for your name,
> and keep us always in your love.

Once again, I am afraid, this is a fiasco, but this time the clockwork driving the wreckage is clearly visible. The translators have evidently shied away from the idea of the fear of the Lord. This unpleasant concept is simply not allowed into the prayer, becoming instead 'unfailing respect', a laughably wet rendering. Impeccable liberal sentiments are at work here, ushering away the notion that God might be fearsome, blinding the translator to the power of the prayer, which urges its hearers to pass beyond fear to the real foundation of our hope, the love of God. In what appears to be a foolish attempt to tidy up the prayer by getting rid of unpleasant pre-conciliar notions like the fear of God, the translator has missed the profounder theological insight and poise of the original, which goes beyond well-meaning liberalism to a wondering sense of the graciousness of God, who establishes us, beyond all fear, in his love. The result in the translation is a prayer of stupefying blandness and emptiness. And here the new draft Sacramentary also lets us down, getting the tone and register of the prayer wrong. Its version runs,

> Lord God teach us to hold your holy name
> both in awe and in lasting affection,
> for you never fail to help and govern
> those whom you establish in your steadfast love.

'Awe' is perhaps not as bad as 'unfailing respect', but it still shies away from fear, and thereby fails to connect with its scriptural sources (try saying to yourself, 'the awe of the Lord is the beginning of wisdom', 'perfect love casts out awe'!). And 'lasting affection' is disastrous, the sort of thing one says one feels for a retiring colleague or a favourite dog. Why ever has the translator not rendered this straightforwardly as 'love'?

The desire to tidy up the prayers of the Missal theologically, removing what were thought to be outdated or non-PC concepts, or to make the prayers more straightforwardly – that is, simplistically – 'biblical', crops up throughout the 1973 translations. The results are not always as disastrous as the example I have just been considering, but I am bound to say that they seem to me hardly ever adequately to match the Latin originals. Take the uncomplicated collect for the tenth Sunday in ordinary time.

> Deus, a quo bona cuncta procedunt,
> tuis largire supplicibus,
> ut cogitimus, te inspirante, quae recta sunt
> et, te gubernante, eadem faciamus.

This is far from brilliant, but it has a neat turn on the idea of putting good thoughts into actual practice. A rough translation might run:

> O God, from whom all good things proceed,
> hear our supplications
> and grant that, inspired by you, we may think right thoughts,
> and guided by you, we may put those thoughts into practice.

The 1973 version of this doesn't even attempt to convey the play on thought and deed here. Instead, it turns the general notion of divine inspiration into the more specific one of the sending of the Holy Spirit, it doodles around with the final clause, sticking in a flourish about peace – an OK concept in 1973, but which has no equivalent in the Latin. In the same way, I don't know where the 'wisdom and love' in the opening invocation comes from.

> God of wisdom and love, source of all good,
> send your Spirit to teach us your truth
> and guide our actions in your way of peace.

This is harmless enough, but notice that the logic of the original has been shot to pieces. In the original prayer God is first identified as the one from whom everything that is good proceeds, and then that general thought is worked out in the second half of the prayer, which explores the particular truth that he is the source even of our rational and moral activity – when we have good thoughts, it is under his inspiration, and when we do act on such thoughts to do good deeds, it is because we are acting under his governance and guidance. This point is actually blunted by turning 'te inspirante' into 'send your Spirit', since it is a much more surprising notion that our innermost (and secular) thoughts spring from God's inspiration than that the Spirit might teach us his truth – which could, after all, take the 'religious' form of reading the scriptures or hearing a sermon or listening to this prayer. In general, the unremarkable original has far more going for it than the jazzed-up translation. The draft Sacramentary, as usual, is very much better here:

> Almighty God, from whom every good gift proceeds
> grant that by your inspiration
> we may discern those things which are right
> and, by your merciful guidance, do them.

It is often in rendering the quieter and less spectacular prayers of the Missal, with their routine-seeming sentiments, that the theological spin of the 1973 translations becomes most evident. Once again, take an unspectacular collect, that for the third Sunday of ordinary time.

> Omnipotens sempiterne Deus,
> dirige actus nostros in beneplacito tuo,
> ut in nomine dilecti Filii tui mereamur
> bonis operibus abundare.

This is a very characteristic Roman prayer, with a very familiar structure – an opening emphasis on the power of God, a plea for his help in which the sovereignty of grace is illustrated in some way, and then a neat turn in which the ideas of our effort and deserving, and God's freely given grace, are paradoxically interwoven. It is not a great prayer, but it is very close indeed to the core ideas of the Roman Liturgy as a whole. A rough version might run

Almighty and everlasting God,
direct our actions in accordance with your will,
so that in the name of your beloved Son,
we may deserve to abound in good works.

As you will see from the inadequacies of my version, this is a
tricky prayer to get just right. 'In accordance with your will'
doesn't quite render 'in beneplacito tuo': it is too effort-bound
and striving. 'So that they may be well-pleasing to your sight' is
archaic but perhaps captures more accurately the element of
gratuitousness which is being begged for. Then there is that
charged word 'mereamur' – the American Jesuit translator
Martin O'Keefe has rendered this 'that we may be privileged to
abound in good works',[11] for which there is a good deal to be
said. But at any rate, the overall drift of the prayer, with its little
play between the notions of God's graciousness and our action,
should be clear enough. The 1973 version is really rather
extraordinary.

All-powerful and ever-living God,
direct your love that is within us,
that our efforts in the name of your Son
may bring mankind to unity and peace.

All sorts of worthy thoughts and fashionably correct sentiments have been imported here. We are no longer praying
for the right direction of our actions, but for the direction of
God's love within us, a concept which I suspect is not entirely
coherent; at any rate I can't make much of it. Even more
strikingly, however, where the original prayer asks, fairly
modestly, that under God's direction we may abound in good
works, the 1973 version asks that 'our efforts ... may bring
mankind to unity and peace', a megalomaniac ambition as
presumptuous as it is unreal, but which, in the context of
the political hopes and fears of the early 1970s, is perhaps
intelligible. This is also, I suppose, the sort of emphasis that
might arise from some of the crasser readings of certain aspects
of *Gaudium et Spes*, but it is certainly no part of the original
prayer. I imagine that another part of the trouble here is that
the translators shied away from the undoubted theological
prickliness of 'mereamur', but what they have ended up with is

a far more starkly Pelagian sentiment than any even hinted at in the original.[12]

Pelagianism again, you see. Or maybe this is too strong a word, for perhaps all it amounts to is a persistent desire to shift the emphasis on to the experiential dimension of religion, to mark out our appropriation of truth rather than God's revelation of it. In the collect for Trinity Sunday, for example, the claim that the Father, by sending the Word of Truth and Spirit of Sanctification – 'admirabile mysterium tuum hominibus declarasti' ('you have declared your wonderful mystery to humankind') – becomes 'Through them we come to know the mystery of your life'. Something of the same tendency is at work in the 'psychologising' of theological concepts elsewhere in the Missal, as in the notorious rendering in Eucharistic Prayer IV of the Johannine phrase 'in finem delixit eos', which represents St John's 'eis telos' – 'he loved them *to the end*' (which carries the meaning of completion, fulfilment, consummation) as 'he showed the depth of his love' – a shift from the profoundly theological towards the sentimentally psychological.

But in any case I don't want to suggest that the translators were *deliberately* introducing Pelagian or other errors into these texts. That they are to be found there is partly the consequence of decisions taken about rhetorical strategy in the translations. The tendency – no, the determination – of the translators to break the complex and tense sentences of the originals into disconnected series of discrete statements often destroys the theological balance as well as the rhythmic and rhetorical structure of the prayers. Again and again the failure to translate the crucial conjunction 'ut' is like pulling the linch-pin joining the carriages of a train. But the fault is not wholly to be laid at the door of the translators. The revision of the actual Latin texts of the Missal for the Missal of Paul VI occasionally shows some of the same sort of theological shifts as those I have been exploring in the 1973 translations. The key example here is the revealing rewriting of the magnificent Gregorian collect formerly prescribed for the fourth Sunday after Pentecost, and now used on the seventeenth Sunday in ordinary time.

This ancient prayer is one of the glories of the Roman liturgical tradition, and it evoked from Cranmer one of his most triumphant translations. I give it first in its ancient, pre-conciliar form.[13]

> Protector in te sperantium Deus
> sine quo nihil est validum, nihil sanctum:
> multiplica super nos misericordiam tuam,
> ut te rectore, te duce,
> sic transeamus per bona temporalia
> ut non ammittamus aeterna.

As I said, this inspired Cranmer to one of his most magnificent efforts, in the Book of Common Prayer collect for the fourth Sunday after Trinity.

> O God, the protector of all that trust in thee,
> without whom nothing is strong, nothing is holy;
> Increase and multiply upon us thy mercy;
> that, thou being our ruler and guide,
> we may so pass through things temporal,
> that we finally lose not the things eternal:
> Grant this, O heavenly Father, for Jesus Christ's sake our Lord.

This is an almost perfect act of translation. Almost, but not quite. The original is profoundly Augustinian, and therefore exquisitely poised. It is a prayer that, ruled and led by God, we may pass through the good things of time, so as not to forfeit eternal life. 'Transeamus per bona temporalia': the world and all that is in it are good, yet we must pass through, 'transeamus', not settle down in it. Cranmer does not render the full paradox, because he doesn't quite render the strength of '*bona* temporalia'. The original is not world-denying, but it emphasises that we are travellers, pilgrims, in a world in which we are not quite at home. That world holds in existence, and is itself good and holy, only because it issues from the hand of God, and its value for us depends on its remaining transparent to him. The whole imagery of the prayer is that of a great journey, carried out under the protection of God, our leader – 'dux' – towards whom we travel in hope, in the world, but not of it.

In the late 1960s, this would not do at all. Sentiments of this sort were held to be life-denying, Manichaean. As a result, the Latin text itself of this ancient prayer was altered.

Protector in te sperantium Deus
sine quo nihil est validum, nihil sanctum:
multiplica super nos misericordiam tuam,
ut te rectore, te duce,
sic bonis transeuntibus nunc utamur
ut iam possimus inhaerere mansuris.

In this version, we no longer pray that we may so pass through the good things of time that we gain the things which are eternal: instead, we pray that we may so make use, here and now, of transient things that, as we do so, we may already lay hold on abiding or permanent things. But note the shift from 'transeamus' to 'utamur'. There is still some tension in the prayer, in the contrast between the transience of the good things we use and the permanence of the good things we hope to inherit, but the theology of the prayer has been radically altered, even contradicted. The eschatological dimension, which in the original involves a journeying towards something not of this world, is now 'cashed', into a laying hold now on permanence. The distinctively Augustinian challenge of the original, that we must simultaneously recognise the goodness of the created world but 'pass through it', is gone. And with it, of course, goes the internal logic of the metaphors of journey, protection, guidance and leading, on which the original was structured, for the prayer is no longer about a journey at all. With the disappearance of 'transeamus', the whole prayer falls apart, the heart has gone out of it.

Here is the 1973 translation, in which these changes in the Latin are even further accentuated:

God our Father and Protector,
without you nothing is holy, nothing has value.
Guide us to everlasting life
by helping us to use wisely the blessings you have given to
    the world.

And here the far more faithful version in the draft Sacramentary brings out more starkly than the 1973 version the nature of the theological transformation which has taken place. The new version runs,

O God, protector of those who hope in you,
without whom nothing is strong, nothing is holy,
enfold us in your gracious care and mercy,
that with you as our ruler and guide
we may wisely use the gifts of this passing world,
and fix our hearts even now on those which last for ever.

Several things have gone wrong here – 'enfold us in your gracious care and mercy', for example, is schmaltzy and overlush, and lacks the concreteness of 'multiplica super nos misericordiam tuam', but it is to the startling phrase which begins the last line – that we may 'fix our hearts even now' – that I would like to draw your attention – a complete rejection of the 'otherworldly' feel of the Gregorian original, and if anything a heightening of the theological mood of a particular moment in the late 1960s.

It is time to draw to a close. The object of this paper has been twofold: to try to indicate some of the characteristic ideas running through the shorter prayers of the Roman Missal, and then to try to assess the extent to which the 1973 English version succeeded in transmitting these ideas, and the theological ethos they represented and encoded. The verdict must be essentially one of sustained failure to rise to the challenge of the Latin, not merely in its great moments, but also in the humdrum bread-and-butter ordinariness of the routine prayers of the Latin propers. I have tried to show that this failure involves more than a simple artistic or literary insensitivity. In almost all cases the distinctive theology of the prayers has been evacuated, and in many cases it has actually been subverted, and replaced by a slacker, often semi-Pelagian theology, far removed from the spirit of the Roman Rite, but redolent of some of the more shallowly optimistic theological currents of the late 1960s.

I hope it has also emerged that an extraordinary proportion of the short collects and related prayers which are the hallmark of the Roman Rite present a uniquely concentrated and balanced theology, distilling the essence of the Latin theological tradition in the patristic and early medieval period. That theology is the birthright of every Roman Catholic, and, as the wonderful Cranmer versions of many of these prayers show, it also underlies much of what we have in common with our Protestant and Anglican fellow-Christians. For fifteen hundred years these prayers encoded a whole theological ethos and piety within the liturgy, yielding their meaning in repeated hearings to anyone who cared to listen attentively to them. Despite their brevity, most of these prayers, even the simplest of them, are nuanced and many-layered, and do in fact repay repeated and close scrutiny.

As will have become clear, the same cannot be said for the English versions which have been in use since 1973. The voice of the collects and related prayers of the Missal, so nuanced, so full of an enlightening theological tension, so charged with a sense of the paradoxes of grace – this was a voice the Church needed in the generation after the Council. It was a voice that was not heard. For a whole generation the splendour of that dimension of the Latin liturgical tradition has been buried behind unworthy and vapid substitutes posing as translation. The seriousness of this substitution can hardly be exaggerated. *Lex orandi, lex credendi*: the balance and nuance of the Latin prayers was a necessary element in the balance and flexibility of theological understanding within the Catholic community. If these model prayers are thin and crude, so will be the people's imagining of God. The collapse of Latin in schools and universities has raised the stakes, for it has meant that the survival of much of our tradition increasingly depends on good translation, and good translation is what we have been denied.

But whatever the reasons, there has been tragic loss. The economy, balance and nuance of the Latin prayers has largely gone from English-speaking Catholic theological culture. The seminaries are full now not only of students with no Latin, but of teachers with no Latin. For them there is simply no direct access to the heart of our theological tradition, the Missal. It is a situation which I confess I find it difficult to think or speak about without bitterness, for this was a loss which was not necessary. Catholics pride themselves on their attentiveness to tradition, but we have come to place the weight of that tradition too much in conformity to the current directives of ecclesiastical authority, too little in the costly and laborious work involved in transmitting the insight and inspiration of the past as a resource for the future. The Missal of 1973 represents a massive and avoidable failure not merely of translation, but a failure of *episkope,* a failure of oversight on the part of those charged with the responsibility of passing on 'the Catholic faith, which comes to us from the Apostles'. The Church is poorer, possibly permanently poorer, because of it.

Of course, one needs to keep a sense of proportion. There is more to liturgy than words, and despite all that I have said, the splendour of the liturgy shines out again and again, even through the drab and imprecise words into which it has so often been rendered. The liturgy nowadays perhaps operates with a narrower range of symbolism and with a smaller repertoire of words, but the average Catholic has a surer grasp of those symbols, and a readier understanding of the words, than was possible before the arrival of the vernacular. Though those touched by the liturgical movement before the Council had access to a marvellous range of bilingual missals, and liturgical commentaries, which opened up some of the riches of the tradition to the educated, Catholic devotional culture in general fed as much or more off paraliturgical and extra-liturgical devotions – the Stations of the Cross, the Rosary – as off the liturgy. Above everything, the scriptures, which the new liturgy has opened up effectively to the laity for the first time in the history of the Church, were a closed book. For all that I have said, therefore, the situation now is very much healthier than it was before the Council.

Moreover, a new translation of the Missal is currently nearing the end of a process of scrutiny by the various English-speaking Episcopal Conferences. As should be clear from the examples I have given you, the new versions have their problems, and will no doubt find their critics. They nevertheless demonstrate throughout a seriousness of engagement with the originals which was almost wholly lacking in 1973. The translators of the new versions certainly seem aware of the intrinsic value of the texts they handle, and more concerned to do justice to both the form and the content of these wonderful prayers. We must wait in hope.

These new translations will help those who wish to do so to go to school to the Roman Rite in the way that the Missal of 1973 not only did not encourage, but actually prevented. But I doubt if they will have the impact they might once have done. We have got out of the habit of attending to the fine detail of such prayers, for in the versions familiar to most people, they did not deserve such attention. It may be that new versions have come not merely a generation late, but a generation too late. The reform of the liturgy has moved on, and there is more between us and these prayers than a twenty-five-year hiccup. The new Sacramentary will not only include the new and very much better translations of the ancient collects I have been considering but, as an alternative to them for every Sunday of the three-year cycle, specially composed English opening prayers which gather up the themes of the day's readings. What I have seen of these prayers is, at one level, extremely encouraging. They seem sensitively put together and in many places rise to real eloquence. There is, moreover, precedent for them in the prayers for the readings in the Easter Vigil. It seems likely that in many parishes, perhaps in most, they will come to displace the ancient collects altogether, as the new Eucharistic Prayers – more of which, I gather, are on the way – have displaced in many parishes the Roman Canon. With these developments, understandable and defensible as they may be, a fundamental move away from a commitment to the pedagogy of tradition, the attentive and prayerful reception of words and rites which have shaped the Church's ethos for almost two millennia, will have been taken. In some important sense, we may be witnessing the dissolution of any coherent sense of a distinctive 'Roman Rite'. For a whole generation, because of the imposition on our worship of shoddy workmanship, we have had to ignore the collects of the Missal, one of the glories and one of the deep resources of our tradition. It would be a supreme irony if, at the very moment at which usable versions of them become officially available, the tide of liturgical change should sweep past them, or even sweep them away.

Notes

This paper was read at the 'Beyond the Prosaic' conference at Westminster College, Oxford, in July 1996. Edited extracts from the paper were printed in *The Tablet* of 6 July 1996, pp. 882–83, and the full text in *New Blackfriars*, January 1997. Reprinted with permission.

1   Edmund Bishop, *Liturgica Historica* (Oxford, 1918), p. 17.

2   Joseph Jungmann, *Pastoral Liturgy* (London, 1962), p. 335.

3   International Commission on English in the Liturgy, *The Sacramentary Segment Three: Order of Mass I* (Aug. 1994), p. 29.

4   For a highly influential discussion of the 'defects' of the Roman Canon, see Cipriano Vagaggini, *The Canon of the Mass and Liturgical Reform*, (London, 1967), pp. 90–107.

5   Vagaggini, *The Canon of the Mass and Liturgical Reform*, p. 88.

6   For convenience, both the Latin texts and the 1973 ICEL versions are taken from *The Gregorian Missal for Sundays* (Solesmes, 1990).

7   'Et recordabor foederis mei vobiscum, et cum omni anima vivente quae carnem vegetat.'

8   The draft Sacramentary here is undistinguished, but once again registers the crucial point:

> Look kindly, Lord, upon our worship and praise,
> that our offering may be acceptable to you,
> and cause us to grow in your love.

The insertion here of 'and cause us' seems to me to weaken but does not obliterate the parallelism with 'sit tibi munus acceptum'.

9   Once again, the draft Sacramentary is an improvement:

> O God, the strength of all who hope in you,
> accept our earnest prayer
> And since without you we are weak and certain to fall,
> grant us always the help of your grace,
> that in following your commands
> we may please you in desire and deed.

If one were minded to quibble, it could be argued that 'weak and certain to fall' is not an exact rendering of the starker 'nihil potest mortalis infirmitas', but the overall success of the translation seems clear.

10   'O Lord, who never fails to help and govern them whom thou dost bring up in thy stedfast fear and love; Keep us, we beseech thee, under the protection of thy good providence, and make us to have a perpetual fear and love of thy holy Name; through Jesus Christ our Lord.'

11   Martin D. O'Keefe, SJ, *Oremus: Speaking with God in the Words of the Roman Rite* (St Louis: Institute of Jesuit Sources, 1973), p. 84.

12   The draft Sacramentary is disappointing here:

> Almighty and eternal God.
> direct all our actions according to your holy will,
> that our lives may be rich in good works,
> done in the name of your beloved Son.

The trouble with this is that 'in nomine dilecti Filii tui' becomes here simply the name in which we do our good works, whereas in the Latin it is because of his name and its saving power that we are *able* to do the good works.

13   I quote the text as edited by H. A. Wilson, *The Gregorian Sacramentary under Charles the Great* (London: Henry Bradshaw Society, 1915), p. 169, but I have modernised the punctuation.

5

Sung Theology: The Liturgical Chant of the Church

MARC-DANIEL KIRBY, O.Cist.

The movement to recover or regenerate important dimensions of the liturgy frequently (and rightly) places great emphasis on the tradition of *sacred music*, and especially chant. I wish to focus here less on the obvious aesthetic appeal of chant than on the neglected topic of its theological function and purpose. And the theological value of liturgical chant might first be approached by means of a definition of terms.[1] Is theology a word *from* God, a word addressed *to* God, or a word *about* God? Is liturgical theology a word received from God by the Church engaged in worship? Is it a word of praise addressed to God by the Church engaged in worship? Is it a word *about* God addressed to the world and emanating from the experience of the Church in worship?

As a word *from* God, liturgical theology may be understood in terms of God's manifestation and revelation of himself and of his will for the salvation of humankind in Christ Jesus, who is 'himself both the mediator and the sum total of revelation'.[2] The mystery of God's self-communication in the historical events of the Incarnation and Paschal Mystery becomes, in the liturgy, an ongoing reality, not in the sense that the liturgy constitutes a new word from God, but in the sense that in the act of the liturgy, the saving Word of God is dynamically present and active.

Understood thus, the principal agent of liturgical theology is God himself, revealing himself in Christ by the power of the Holy Spirit within the act of the liturgy. Such a 'liturgical theology from above' is strongly Trinitarian.

As a word *to* God, theology may be understood in terms of the human response to God's self-revelation in the saving deeds of the Incarnation and Paschal Mystery. Such a response, springing out of the communal rememoration of God's wondrous deeds, is necessarily doxological and eucharistic. That this articulation of praise and thanksgiving by a liturgical assembly is itself intrinsically theological may be verified as much by a reading of the Anaphora of Saint Basil as by a perusal of the prefaces of the Roman Missal. Insofar as the liturgy 'is rightly seen as an exercise of the priestly office of Jesus Christ' and 'an action of Christ the Priest and of his Body, which is the Church', the agent of liturgical theology, the *liturgical theologian*, is none other than the total Christ himself, Head and members united in the Holy Spirit.[3] Liturgical theology, understood in this way, is strongly Christological and ecclesiological.

As a word *about* God, liturgical theology may be understood in terms of the experiential knowledge of the economic Trinity, which is the fruit of 'that full, conscious and actual participation in liturgical celebrations which is demanded by the very nature of the liturgy'.[4] While the act of liturgy is primarily doxological and not didactic, the didactic dimension of the liturgy cannot be ignored nor can it be disassociated from the specifically educative action of the Holy Spirit within the Church, according to the words of Christ: 'When the Spirit of truth comes, he will guide you into all truth' (John: 16:13). The liturgy is in fact the Church's 'word about God' addressed to her children as well as to the world, a word inspired by the Spirit of truth, who proceeds from the Father, and bears witness to Christ (cf. John 15:26–27). In this instance, the *liturgical theologian* is the *Ecclesia Orans*, the Church, guided by the Holy Spirit 'into all truth' (John 16:13), even as she engages in the act of worship. Such a liturgical theology is at once pneumatological and ecclesiological.

Liturgical theology cannot be identified with only one of the three approaches presented above, for the liturgy itself is, organically and simultaneously, a word *from* God, a word *to* God and a word *about* God. Liturgical chant occurs when this word is sung within the context of the liturgical action. Priority is necessarily given to the word *from* God, for it is God's self-revelation and self-communication, by means of a complexus of sacred signs operative within the liturgy, that generates the word *to* God. It is the word *to* God that unfolds experientially as a word *about* God. Understood in this way, the enactment of the liturgy is intrinsically theological. The liturgical event itself is the source, the matrix and the expression of theology. Theology 'emerges from the font of liturgical experience'.[5]

Without referring to the controversies concerning the origins of Christian liturgical chant, it is both possible and useful to formulate a negative description of it. Liturgical chant does not 'accompany' the *actio*; it is an integral part of it. It is neither ornament nor embellishment. Liturgical chant is not an autonomous element, independent of its ritual context.

> Music is not a conjunct to worship. It is the way the Church worships. Music is neither supplementary to, nor an enrichment of worship. It is the expression of worship itself. It is not an accompaniment, a background, a preparation, a moodsetter, a filler, or any such thing, and it is certainly not a *divertimento*.[6]

Unlike religious music and popular religious song, liturgical chant cannot stand independently of the total liturgical action without its meaning becoming obscured. The meaning of a *Sanctus*, for example, is essentially theological and liturgical, not musical. Its theological and liturgical meaning is revealed only in the wider context of the whole Eucharistic Prayer. A *Gradual* chant is related to the hearing of the Word of God to which it responds, an *Alleluia* to the Holy Gospel which it welcomes and announces.

Described positively, chant is purely vocal music. It arises from the words of the liturgical texts and cannot be separated from them. 'The origin of the melody is found in the word.'[7] Appropriated by the liturgy, the chanted word is ritually adapted to 'what no eye has seen, nor ear heard, nor the heart of man conceived' (1 Corinthians 2:9). Lossky writes: 'In the Orthodox tradition, both Eastern and Western, the music is provided by chant. Consequently, it is closely linked to the word; it is at the service of the word; it is the vehicle of the word.'[8]

Chant articulates the words of the liturgical texts and allows them to resonate harmoniously with other symbolic elements of the *actio* in such a way as to disclose their specifically theological value. The function of liturgical chant is to dilate the sacred text and render it more penetrating 'until we make contact with the Presence with which the texts are filled'.[9] The Church perceives the mystery of the living Word of God expressed in the human words of Scripture as analogous to the mystery of the Incarnation in which the Word of the Eternal Father took on himself the flesh of human weakness.[10] The analogy can be pursued so as to see in the chant melodies (cantilenas) of the liturgy a kind of vesture for the Word.[11] The vesture has no movement of itself; it is animated from within by the Word whom it reveals, conceals, adorns and prolongs. Maurice Zundel writes: 'It was a natural development when in the liturgy the sacred texts put on the garb of song, and music sought to render the Divine atmosphere with which the words are invested.'[12]

The theological and spiritual function of liturgical chant is intimately tied to the threefold definition of liturgical theology elucidated above. In the liturgy, chant becomes a vehicle of liturgical theology as word *from* God, word *to* God and word *about* God. Liturgical chant is at the service of the word *from* God: the principal agent of the liturgy, God himself, revealing himself in Christ by the power of the Holy Spirit within the *actio*. Functioning in this capacity, liturgical chant may be described as *epiphanic*. Liturgical chant is equally at the service of the word *to* God: the action of Christ the Priest and of his Body, the Church, engaged in the glorification of the Father in the unity of the Holy Spirit. Functioning in this capacity, liturgical chant may be described as *doxological* and *eucharistic*. Finally, liturgical chant serves the word *about* God: the Gospel proclaimed to the world, and the edifying word by which the Holy Spirit forms and teaches the Church engaged in worship. Functioning in this capacity, liturgical chant may be described as *catechetical* and *mystagogical*. Liturgical chant is wholly at the service of liturgical theology and has an intrinsically theological value.

The musical forms of liturgical chant emerge from the various liturgical texts and from their function and place within the sacred action. The texts themselves are organically related to their liturgical context, to the feast or mystery celebrated, and to the significance of a given moment or movement within the enactment of the liturgy. Liturgical chant thus serves a ritual function; its meaning, however, is, ultimately, theological and spiritual.

Chant is an integral part of the liturgical action; as such it refers to and reveals the mystery, influencing and shaping the spiritual life of individual worshippers and of a community. The analysis of liturgical chant as music *tout court* will fall short of the mark, 'for while a chant may be discussed and dissected ... as an object of study in itself, it must not be forgotten that it was composed in the creation of a complete way of life, the performance of the *opus Dei*, the work of God'.[13]

Religious music and popular religious song offer a window into the soul of the individual composer, revealing the composer's personal experience of God or of the mysteries of the faith. In contrast, the composer of liturgical chant traditionally remains anonymous; liturgical chant is a window not into the soul of any one individual, but into the soul of the Church. As 'sung theology', liturgical chant reveals, transmits and serves the orthodox vision of the mysteries of the faith within the context of their sacramental actualisation by the Church.

In the liturgical traditions of both East and West, the *actio* privileges the use of chant, 'a mysterious combination of verbal-linguistic expression and non-verbal vocalization'.[14] Chant is to the ear what a sacred image is to the eye: a sensible mediation of a spiritual reality. The analogy is suggested by St John Damascene:

> The apostles saw Christ in the flesh: they witnessed his sufferings and his miracles, and heard his words. We too desire to see, and to hear, and so be filled with gladness. They saw him face to face, since he was physically present. Since he is no longer physically present, we hear his words read from books and by hearing our

souls are sanctified and filled with blessing, and so we worship, honouring the books from which we hear his words.[15]

Chant prepares, accompanies and expresses the Church's experience of Christ in the liturgy, an experience mediated by words and by a complexus of other sacred signs. Kevin Irwin astutely remarks that the proper interpretation of liturgical texts requires understanding the kind of chant melodies assigned to these texts, not just the words of the texts.[16] Carrying Irwin's insight further yet, it may be said that the proper interpretation of all liturgical texts requires that they be sung in their proper liturgical form and expression, and heard in their native liturgical context. According to St John Damascene, by hearing *in this way,* 'our souls are sanctified and filled with blessing, and so, we worship'.[17] This double work of sanctification and worship is accomplished in the Church by the presence of the Risen Christ and the operation of the Holy Spirit; 'there is a twofold movement, a back and forth play, in which the Father communicates self through Christ in the Spirit (*katabatic*) so that the "many" may freely give themselves back (*anabatic)* in love to receive God's gift'.[18]

The vast majority of liturgical chants are drawn directly from the Scriptures, and principally from the psalter. In these chants, Christ is present either as the one addressing the Father, as the one addressing the Church, or as the one to whom the Church addresses her supplications and her praise.[19] In the first case, Christ sings with the Church, facing the Father; in the second, as the revelation of the Father's glory, he sings to the Church, facing her; in the third, it is Christ who receives the song of the Church, as the object of her contemplation and desire.[20] In reading the Scriptures, the Church recognises the voice of Christ; hearing the Scriptures, she confesses his presence.[21]

In both Jewish and Christian tradition, chant is the normal medium for the liturgical proclamation of Holy Scripture.[22] By means of simple melodic formulae, adapted to the punctuation, accents and cadences of the text, the word is presented audibly, intelligibly and objectively. Not only does the ritual cantillation of the text reduce the need for artificial amplification of the voice; it lifts the text above the personal, the subjective and the informative, and disposes the hearers to experience its mysterious power: the presence of Christ and the action of the Holy Spirit.[23]

Euchological texts, entrusted to the presider (and at times to the deacon), receive a musical treatment not unlike that of the readings. Joseph Gélineau describes the cantillation of the presider:

> The pre-eminence of the celebrant's song finds expression in the music which is the vehicle of his prayer. . . . He makes no pretensions to be a virtuoso. Just a few notes, a few melodic formulas which are restrained in character and fixed by law serve him in his prayer or thanksgiving. Here is no exercise of the fine arts, but only the perfection of practical art in the mouth of the 'sacrificer', that is, the 'artisan of the sacred'.[24]

The presider, the *artisan of the sacred*, serves most effectively when he makes use of his voice as the human means by which the prayer and thanksgiving of the total Christ, Head and members, ascends to the Father, in the Holy Spirit. The liturgy strikes at the root of individualistic piety and subjective interpretation by obliging the presider to engage in dialogue with the assembly, to play in the plural *we*, and to solicit repeatedly the assent of the people, expressed by *Amen*. The simple, hieratic cantillations of the various liturgical traditions invite the presider to humble service of the mysteries and to iconic transparency.

The theological function of liturgical chant in these diverse forms is threefold. It is *ecclesiological* in so far as it serves the unity of the Body of Christ by binding its members to one another and to their Head. It is *sacramental* in that it serves the actualisation of Christ's mysteric presence in the midst of the assembly by functioning as the human vehicle of his word to the Church, and of his prayer to the Father, in the Holy Spirit. Finally, it is *eschatological* because it causes the Church to 'incline the ear of her heart' (Psalm 44:11) to the 'voice of a great multitude, like the sound of many waters' (Revelation 19:6), the sound of the glorious and eternal *leitourgia* celebrated in the heavenly Jerusalem.[25]

It is especially by virtue of its sacramental and eschatological functions that liturgical chant illustrates the great law of the sacramental economy set in motion by the Incarnation. St John

Damascene refers explicitly to the 'perceptible words' of the Church's prayer and psalmody in this regard:

> Just as we physically listen to perceptible words in order to understand spiritual things, so also by using bodily sight we reach spiritual contemplation. For this reason Christ assumed both soul and body, since man is fashioned from both. Likewise baptism is both of water and of Spirit. It is the same with communion, prayer, psalmody, candles or incense; they all have a double significance, physical and spiritual.[26]

Created matter, including the human body and its senses, is not excluded from Christ's sanctifying work nor from his Church's glorification of the Father in spirit and in truth. Matter, on the contrary, is foundational to the whole sacramental economy because, in the words of St John Damascene, 'the Creator of matter became matter for my sake, willed to take his abode in matter, and worked out my salvation through matter'.[27]

Liturgical chant is often described as immaterial; it is in fact material in so far as it is inseparable from the ordered sound of speech. It is a heightened form of language. Chant's raw material, vocal sound, 'is readily at hand from the beginnings of human life, and is supple and adaptable for the elaboration of symbols expressing all nuances of human insight and conception'.[28] Apparently evanescent, chant in fact perdures in the memory long after being heard or sung. Liturgical chant depends on the word of Scripture, rearticulates and, at the same time, transfigures it, rendering it more apt for its specifically sacramental and eschatological functions within the *actio*.

Liturgical chant is more than a straightforward delivery of a sacred text. In order to fulfil its sacramental and eschatological function, chant effects a certain estrangement from what is familiar, a transcendence of the utilitarian criteria of secular functionalism. This transcendence is achieved by means of creative obedience to an ensemble of musical canons, developed over the course of time by the diverse liturgical traditions of the Church, and tested by a long experience of liturgical practice.

The canons of liturgical chant foster, promote and protect its specifically theological function within the *actio*. They discern between authentic artistic creativity and the tyranny of subjective fantasy, while offering the artist – composer or singer – a certain number of musical formulae to be used in various combinations, thereby assuring what Kovalevsky calls 'a character of coherent continuity, universality and variety'.[29] Fidelity to these canons, something not incompatible with their adaptation to various cultures and historical contexts, forges a link of continuity between succeeding generations of worshippers.

Liturgical chant arises out of a reading, or better yet, a hearing of the archetypical Word, and the interiorisation of musical prototypes with a liturgical tradition. The hieratic quality of liturgical chant is an anthropological expression of the transcendent common to many cultures.[30] Liturgical chant cannot be a naturalistic echo of 'the form of this world which is passing away' (1 Corinthians 7:31); its essential function is not to cause aesthetic pleasure, nor to entertain, but to show forth symbolically, by anticipation, the eternal realities of the Kingdom.[31] Fidelity to the eschatological and sacramental functions of liturgical chant oblige its artisans to obey what one author has called the *psaltic canon*.[32]

The Church is otherworldly, even as she is sent by Christ into the world; her liturgy is otherworldly even as it is enacted in space and time 'for the life of the world' (John 6:51).[33] The liturgy draws its means of expression from the various resources of human culture. These means are nonetheless subjected to purification and refinement – to transfiguration in the fire of the Holy Spirit – in view of the proper end of the liturgy itself: the manifestation of the Kingdom of God.[34] Liturgical art cannot fulfil its sacramental function unless it is worldly; it cannot fulfil its eschatological function unless it is otherworldly. 'They are not of the world, even as I am not of the world. . . . As thou didst send me into the world, so I have sent them into the world' (John 17:16, 18). The intelligibility of liturgical signs is contingent upon their worldliness; the *iconicity* of liturgical signs is contingent upon their other-worldliness.[35]

The Church, and especially the Church engaged in the enactment of the liturgy, reveals the Kingdom of God in the world
and to the world. Christ and his Church, acting synergetically in
the Holy Spirit, are the sacrament of salvation in the world, the
gift of salvation offered to the world for the glory of the Father.

> It is of the essence of the Church to be both human and divine,
> visible yet endowed with invisible resources, eager to act yet intent
> upon contemplation, present in this world yet not at home in it;
> and the Church is all these things in such wise that in her the
> human is directed and subordinated to the divine, the visible
> likewise to the invisible, action to contemplation, and this present
> world to that city yet to come which we seek.[36]

The soteriological and doxological dimensions of the liturgy
are best perceived when the sacramental means employed by
the Church are seen as belonging to her in a special way, and as
proceeding from what is divine in her as well as from what is
human, from her heavenly and her earthly nature.

Chant is an integral part of the liturgy because the liturgy is,
by its very nature, 'a complexus of sacred signs'.[37] Singing is not
an adjunct to the liturgy; in both East and West the sung celebration is its normative form. Contextualised by the other
elements of the *actio*, and resonating with them, an optimal use
of chant can open minds and hearts to the knowledge of God
and to an anticipated experience, a foretaste, of the Kingdom.

The liturgy in its various manifestations exists for no other
reason than to constitute and sustain the life of the Church as a
participation *here and now* in the life of the Most Holy Trinity
there and then. 'The liturgy leads us out toward Eternity.'[38] This
mysteric participation in the life of the Triune God is prayer,
the very life-breath of the Church. Consequently, prayer is the
principal functional criterion of liturgical art in all of its forms:
chant, iconography, architecture and bodily movement.[39]
Everything therefore in liturgical chant must serve, foster and
express prayer: the prayer uniting the total Christ to the Father,
and the prayer of the Church uniting her to Christ. Every form
of musical artistry alien to 'the peace of God which surpasses
understanding' (Philippians 4:7), the seal of true prayer, is
incompatible with the function of liturgical chant.

Liturgical chant is woven into the very fabric of the liturgy; to excise it from its liturgical context violates its very nature and leaves the *lex agendi* theologically threadbare and incomplete.[40] Lossky observes that music is not 'an additional ornament in the liturgy, something added as an extra for the sake of beauty. Music in the liturgy is not an autonomous element; it is not a separate element, an element on its own.'[41] Within the context of the *actio,* liturgical chant is a constitutive element of the *lex orandi.* Outside of that context, the theological significance of liturgical chant cannot adequately be appreciated or interpreted.

Specifically Christian liturgical music is marked by three characteristics: breath, interiority and freedom. The breath of God is the very transmission of life. 'The Lord God formed man of dust from the ground, and breathed into his nostrils the breath of life; and man became a living being' (Genesis 2:7). The breath of God cannot be dissociated from his word, and the word of God cannot be uttered save in a communication of his breath.

By breathing and by speaking, the human being expresses likeness to God. Jesus says: 'The words that I have spoken to you are spirit and life' (John 6:63). Thus, breath, life and word constitute an inseparable triad in the divine economy of creation and redemption. In the Christian tradition, breath and word are invested with a Trinitarian significance; they become symbolic of Spirit and Word. St Irenaeus writes: 'The Spirit manifests the Word but the Word articulates the Spirit.'[42] The Father reveals himself and draws man into the circle of divine life by means of the Spirit and the Word. Similarly, by means of breath and word, man 'confesses with his lips' (Romans 10:10), 'calls upon the name of the Lord' (Romans 10:13), and 'sings psalms and hymns and spiritual songs' (Colossians 3:16). Breath and word are the indispensable human components of liturgical chant; Spirit and Word together constitute liturgical chant's divine archetype.

Interiority, the second characteristic of Christian liturgical chant, is also characteristic of the Kingdom of God. The seed is sowed in the earth, the leaven hidden in the flour, the treasure hidden in the field (cf. Matthew 13:31, 33, 44). The

Kingdom of God is not achieved by means of laws imposed from without; it erupts from within, 'a spring of water welling up to eternal life' (John 4:14). So, too, with prayer: its vital principle is interior, where the Spirit intercedes with sighs too deep for words (cf. Romans 8:9, 26). Unlike the music of the ancient Greeks, which sought to harmonise itself with the external forces of the universe, Christian liturgical chant begins within, where the human spirit is attuned to the Spirit of God, 'the Spirit himself bearing witness with our spirit' (Romans 8:16).[43]

The preaching of the Gospel links freedom, the third characteristic of Christian liturgical chant, to truth. 'If you continue in my word, you are truly my disciples, and you will know the truth, and the truth will make you free' (John 8:31–32). In the Christian dispensation, knowledge of the truth is a gift freely given by God in Christ and assimilated progressively by the believer. The place of this progressive assimilation is the cyclical and repetitive enactment of the liturgy. In the liturgy the heart feeds upon truth as upon a nourishment provided by God and so grows in freedom.[44] Chant helps to 'calm, elevate and purify the most secret regions of the soul',[45] preparing it to be penetrated and transformed by the Spirit of Truth who guides into all truth (cf. John 16:13). The spiritual resonance of Christian liturgical chant is proportionate to the subject's inner adhesion to the truth of Christ, sent to proclaim release to captives and to set at liberty those who are oppressed (cf. Luke 4:18). At the same time, by confronting both singers and hearers with the Word of truth, liturgical chant is an agent of ongoing spiritual liberation or conversion.

The relationship between breath and word, the interior impulse of filial prayer in the Holy Spirit, and the interplay between the assent to truth and growth in freedom are theological realities emanating from the heart of the Gospel and resonating in every enactment of the liturgy. To com-municate, assimilate, sustain, and propagate these realities, a new art was born, an indispensable complement of the *kerygma:* Christian liturgical chant. In response to these and to other exigencies of the developing liturgy, Christian liturgical chant, in both form and performance, came to be associated with a certain number of musical characteristics. Five of these characteristics will be studied here.

The first pertains to the irreplaceable value of the human voice in the liturgy. Only the human voice, a coincidence of breath and word, can express directly the inner movements of the heart. Clement of Alexandria offers a profoundly theological justification for the absolute primacy accorded the human voice in Christian worship:

> The Word of God, scorning the lyre and cithara as lifeless instruments, and having rendered harmonious by the Holy Spirit both this cosmos and even man the microcosm, made up of body and soul – he sings to God on his many-voiced instrument and he sings to man, himself an instrument: 'You are my cithara, my aulos and my temple', a cithara because of harmony, an aulos because of spirit, and a temple because of the word, so that the first might strum, the second might breathe, and the third might encompass the Lord. . . . The Lord made man a beautiful breathing instrument after his own image; certainly he is himself an all-harmonious instrument of God, well-tuned and holy, the transcendental wisdom, the heavenly Word.[46]

The human person created in the image and likeness of the Word is, like the Word, 'a beautiful breathing instrument', destined by the Father 'to the praise of his glorious grace' (Ephesians 1:6).[47] Historically, the exclusion of musical instruments from the liturgy proceeds not only from the Church's desire to banish from her cult anything redolent of worldly entertainment, but also from a lofty theological anthropology.[48] 'The notes previously observed as issuing from musical instruments are now seen to emanate from the rational bodies of men.'[49]

Liturgical chant is sung speech; this is a second characteristic. It is not the application of a pre-established music, composed of independently determined notes and rhythms, to a text. Liturgical chant is not a question of 'words for the music' but rather of 'music for the words' or of 'music *in* the words', for the cantilena is born of the text itself. The precise and intelligible communication of liturgical texts within the worshipping assembly requires an accurate and objective vocal delivery.

Objectivity is the third characteristic of liturgical chant. Even in its more ornate forms, cantillation remains a technique of oral communication 'at the service of the word and of the community, whose free access to the word must be respected to the uttermost degree'.[50] Objectivity pertains not only to the naked text but to its theological meaning as well. Ordinary speech is an inadequate vehicle of the oral tradition which transmits not only the sacred text but its theological meaning as well. The liturgical cantilena espouses a fixed cursus of accents and emphases, thereby delivering the text in an objective manner and disclosing the way in which the liturgical tradition has heard and prayed the text in the past.

Traditional chant formulae may be described as both hallowed and hallowing; holiness is a fourth characteristic. Chant is hallowed by reason of its intimate association with the Word of God and by centuries of use in 'the assembly of the saints' (Psalm 149:1). Kept alive in the collective memory of the Church, it hallows both singer and hearer by fostering the assimilation of the sacred text and by serving as a sign and bond of communion with the saints. In the enactment of the liturgy, chant is a sacred doorway to the numinous. As a sacramental expression of ecclesial prayer, liturgical chant must mediate and express the encounter with the Holy.

The creative reconfiguration of set musical patterns, adapted to the form and theological meaning of the word, forms within the memory of the subject a store of associations with previously assimilated experiences of the Holy. The simplest melodic formula has strong evocative power capable of 'opening a door through which Mystery approaches the creature, and the creature moves out in response'.[51] The first few notes of the *Exultet* intoned at the Paschal Vigil suffice to evoke the glory of the Paschal Mystery in the hearts of the hearers.[52] The same may be said of other chants repeated year after year at fixed moments in the liturgical cycle. Each repetition of the symbolic word is thereby contextualised and recontextualised in an ever-deepening perception of the *theologia prima* that reaches from one generation of saints to the next.

The fifth characteristic of liturgical chant is that it fosters active and conscious participation in the *actio* by engaging the

assembly in both listening and singing. The attribution of
various forms of liturgical chant to the presider, deacon,
psalmist or cantor, schola, and assembly is neither arbitrary nor
optional; it pertains to the essential nature of the liturgy as a
corporate act of the whole Christ, Head and members.

The cantillation of euchological texts, of readings and of
psalmody invites the assembly to listen actively. Simple and
adaptable musical formulae of cantillation have withstood the
test of time in diverse liturgical traditions, not only because of
their intrinsic artistic value, but also because of their proven
ritual functionality. They effectively stimulate active and
intentional listening.[53]

The chants of the assembly require a cantilena that springs
from the liturgical texts themselves and expresses their natural
verbal inflections by means of simple musical formulae adapted
to the specific liturgical function of each piece.[54] A composition
that does not belong to the liturgy and lead more deeply into
the mystery celebrated, even though it be sung with full-voiced
enthusiasm by all, cannot be qualified a true expression of
conscious and active participation in the liturgical action.[55]
Active participation implies that the assembly is singing the
liturgy itself, beginning with the dialogical chants, acclamations
and refrains.[56]

Unlike standard hymn-singing, the performance of which is
relatively uniform and congregational, liturgical chant privileges the responsorial, dialogical, antiphonal and acclamatory
modes of performance. These, being among the most effective
forms of active sung participation, manifest more adequately
the mystery of the Church as a eucharistic organism of different
members characterised by 'the order of symphony, an order in
liberty and in love'.[57]

Can liturgical chant be called sung theology? Undeniably,
liturgical chant plays a role in generating liturgical theology.
Prosper Guéranger, Lambert Beauduin, Aemiliana Löhr,
Alexander Schmemann and other luminaries of the liturgical
movement give evidence of the theological significance of
liturgical chant in their lives and in their writings. More
fundamentally however, because chant is integral to the
complexus of sacred signs called into play by the *actio,* when it is

sung and heard by believers within the liturgical context, where it resonates with other signs, it becomes a privileged expression of *theologia prima.* Within the complete context of the liturgy, chant is a vehicle and expression of the word *from* God, the word *to* God and the word *about* God.

This specifically theological value of liturgical chant includes its epiphanic, doxological, eucharistic, catechetical and mystagogical dimensions. Liturgical chant sung, heard and understood in this way contributes to the edification of the Church in unity, to the knowledge of the 'unsearchable riches' of Christ (Ephesians 3:8), and to the experience of things unseen, 'the things that are eternal' (2 Corinthians 4:18).

The Church prays with human breath and human words. In the liturgy, these are joined to the Holy Spirit and to the Word of God. More, however, is required than the mere vocalisation of a sacred text. Chant demands of the subject a capacity for silence and for listening. 'In the articulation of the text . . . the singer must be intensely active, and in the silence between the phrases or verses, attentive in silence, in a sense contemplative.'[58] As sung theology, chant is *apophatic* in its silences and *cataphatic* in its delivery of the word.[59]

> Rather than thinking of the chant as a 'schola cantorum', or 'school of singers', we might think of it as a school, so to speak, of 'sacred speaking', designed to guide us into a way of 'saying' the texts directed by a deeper intelligence within us, an intelligence capable of being aware of the divine source of what we are saying. This sacred speaking arises out of a delicate relationship within us between silence and the word. It is, in a sense, 'contemplative speech'.[60]

To say that chant is a school of *sacred speaking* is to recognise its potential as a primary theological source. Authentic liturgical chant is a work of the people. It is 'proletarian, communitarian and quotidian'.[61] For chant to be experienced effectively as a primary theological source, for it to be assimilated in the *lex credendi* and bear fruit in the *lex vivendi*, it must be practised consistently and repeatedly as the normal form of communitarian worship. When chant is perceived as a means of 'solemnisation' and not as the quotidian and habitual way of enacting the liturgy, the full impact of its theological value is weakened.[62]

As the habitual and normative expression of liturgical prayer, the sturdy simplicity of chant withstands continual and repeated performance without becoming old and wearisome. It eschews musical accompaniment; the only instrument necessary is the human voice. Its fundamental principle of interpretation is the primacy of word over music. As an integral part of the liturgy, chant is a channel and vehicle of the Word of God, of the prayer of Christ, and of the thanksgiving of the Church; it is both sanctified and sanctifying. Finally, liturgical chant is participatory theology; by its simplicity, as well as by the diversity of its forms, it draws all the members of a worshipping assembly – *cantantes, legentes* and *audientes* – into the *actio,* and, by means of the *actio,* into the Mystery.

Notes

1 Cf. Kevin Irwin's discussion of the work of Anselm Stolz on the meaning of *theologia,* in *Context and Text: Method in Liturgical Theology* (Collegeville, MN: Liturgical Press, 1994), p. 266.

2 Vatican II, Dogmatic Constitution on Divine Revelation *Dei Verbum* (DV), Article 2.

3 Vatican II, Constitution on the Sacred Liturgy *Sacrosanctum Concilium* (SC), Article 7.

4 SC, Article 14.

5 Archimandrite Vasileios, *Hymn of Entry: Liturgy and Life in the Orthodox Church,* trans. Elizabeth Briere (Crestwood, NJ: St Vladimir's Seminary Press, 1984), p. 11.

6 Sergei Glagolev, 'An Introduction to the Interpretation of Liturgical Music', *Orthodox Church Music* 1 (1983), p. 25.

7 Marie Pierik, *Dramatic and Symbolic Elements in Gregorian Chant* (New York: Desclée Company, 1963), p. 13. Pierik's use of the word *melody* is technically inexact. Stravinsky writes: 'The term *melody* in the scientific meaning of the word, is applied to the top voice in polyphony, thus differentiating melody from the unaccompanied cantilena that is called *monody*' ('Poetics of Music in the Form of Six Lessons', in Kevin Irwin, *Context and Text: Method in Liturgical Theology,* Collegeville, MN: Liturgical Press, 1994, p. 41). This being said for the sake of technical precision, in this work, *melody* and *melodic* will occasionally be used as Dr Pierik has used them: to refer to the unaccompanied cantilena that characterises chant.

8   N. Lossky, 'Some Thoughts on Liturgical Music', *Orthodox Church Music* 1 (1983), p. 5.

9   Maurice Zundel, *The Splendour of the Liturgy* (London: Sheed & Ward, 1945), p. 78.

10 DV, Article 13.

11 The *General Instruction of the Roman Missal*, Article 306, says concerning sacred vesture: 'The beauty of a vestment should derive from its material and design rather than from lavish ornamentation.' Might we not say as much of sacred melodies? Vulgar harmonisations, strident accompaniments and sentimentally charged executions do little to conceal a piece which is badly composed and structured in the first place.

12 Zundel, *The Splendour of the Liturgy*, p. 285.

13 David Hiley, *Western Plainchant: A Handbook* (Oxford: Clarendon Press, 1993), p. 7.

14 Phillip Harnoncourt, 'Te Deum Laudamus', in Angelus A. Häussling (ed.), *The Meaning of the Liturgy*, trans. Linda M. Mahoney (Collegeville, MN: Liturgical Press, 1994), p. 96.

15 St John of Damascene, *On the Divine Images*, trans. David Anderson (Crestwood, NJ: St Vladimir's Seminary Press, 1980), p. 72. The word 'read' should not mislead us. 'To read' has a technical meaning in ancient liturgical sources. It refers to chanted declamation, better termed 'cantillation'. See Joseph Gélineau, *Chant et musique dans le culte chrétien* (Paris: Editions Fleurus, 1962), p. 77.

16 Irwin, *Context and Text*, p. 59.

17 St John Damascene, *On the Divine Images*, p. 72.

18 Edward J. Kilmartin, *Christian Liturgy: Theology and Practice, I. Systematic Theology of Liturgy* (Kansas City, MO: Sheed & Ward, 1988), p. 90.

19 'Praesens adest in denique dum supplicat et psallit Ecclesia, ipse qui promisit: "Ubi sunt duo vel tres congregati in nomine meo, ibi sum in medio eorum" (Matthew 18:20).' SC, Article 7.

20 The use of titles, orations and antiphons in conjunction with the psalter attests to the Christological illumination of the psalms traditional in the Church's liturgical prayer and authorised by the Risen Christ himself in Luke 24:44: 'Everything written *about me* in the law of Moses and the prophets and the psalms must be fulfilled.' See Balthasar Fischer, 'Le Christ dans les psaumes', *La Maison-Dieu* 27 (1951), pp. 86–113; Claude Jean-Nesmy, *La Tradition médite le psautier chrétien* (Paris: Editions Téqui, 1973); A. Rose, *Les Psaumes, voix du Christ et de l'Eglise* (Paris: Lethielleux, 1981).

21 In the present revised Roman Rite, this is expressed by the acclamations which frame the proclamation of the Gospel: *Laus tibi, Christe* and *Gloria tibi, Domine.*

22 See Gélineau, *Chant et musique dans le culte chrétien*, p. 77.

23 'The Scriptures, and above all in their liturgical proclamation, are the
    source of life and power. . . . When this word is proclaimed in the
    Church and put into living practice, it enlightens the faithful through
    the working of the Holy Spirit and draws them into the entire mystery
    of the Lord as a reality to be lived': 'General Introduction to the Order
    of Readings for Mass', Article 47, in *Lectionary*, vol. 1 (London:
    HarperCollins, 1993), p. xxviii.

24 Gélineau, *Chant et musique dans le culte chrétien*, p. 74.

25 'The earthly liturgy can be described as a foretaste of the heavenly liturgy.
    It is the expression of an anticipated reality. It is the enactment of the
    desire or hope for something that already exists elsewhere. But it is also a
    real participation in the heavenly liturgy. . . . The earthly liturgy is directed
    to the heavenly liturgy, and obtains its basic orientation from it': Kilmartin,
    Christian Liturgy, p. 91.

26 St John Damascene, *On the Divine Images*, pp. 72–73.

27 Ibid., p. 23.

28 William A. Van Roo, 'Symbol in Art and Sacraments', in *Symbolisme et
    théologie* (Rome: Editrice Anselmiana, 1974), p. 154.

29 '[U]n caractère de pérennité, d'universalité et de variété dans la
    cohérence': C. Kovalevsky, 'Le Chant de la liturgie chrétienne', in *Liturgies
    de l'église particulière et liturgie de l'église universelle* (Rome: Edizioni
    Liturgiche, 1976), pp. 183–94, at p. 184.

30 See Peter Jeffery, 'Chant East and West: Toward a Renewal of the Tradi-
    tion', in David Power, Mary Collins and Mellonee Burnim (eds.), *Music
    and the Experience of God* (Edinburgh: T&T Clark, 1989), p. 28.

31 On the liturgy as the symbolic epiphany of the Kingdom, see
    A. Schmemann, *The Eucharist* (Crestwood, NY: St Vladimir's Seminary
    Press, 1988), pp. 27–48.

32 Marcel Pirard-Angistriotu, 'Le Chant liturgique orthodoxe entre la
    polyphonie et la monophonie', *Contact* (1995), p. 193.

33 See A. Kavanagh, *On Liturgical Theology* (New York: Pueblo, 1984), pp. 3–
    69. See also A. Schmemann, *For the Life of the World* (Crestwood, NY: St
    Vladimir's Seminary Press, 1973), pp. 11–22.

34 See Zundel, *The Splendour of the Liturgy*, p. 283.

35 On the quality of liturgical *iconicity*, see Giancarlo Carminati, 'Una teoria
    semiologica del linguaggio liturgico', in *Ephemerides Liturgicae* 3 (May–June
    1988), pp. 184–207.

36 SC, Article 2.

37 C. Vagaggini, *Theological Dimensions of the Liturgy* (Collegeville, MN:
    Liturgical Press, 1976), p. 27.

38 Evelyn Underhill, *The Mystery of Sacrifice: A Meditation on the Liturgy*
    (London: Longmans, Green & Co., 1938), p. xiv.

39   Nicolas Ozoline, 'L'Icône, analogie et complémentarité de l'image par rapport au geste et à la parole liturgique', in *Gestes et paroles dans les diverses familles liturgiques,* ed. Constantin Andronikof (Rome, 1978), p. 77.

40   On the *lex agendi,* see Irwin, *Context and Text,* p. 55.

41   Lossky, 'Some Thoughts on Liturgical Music', p. 4.

42   St Irenaeus of Lyons, *Proof of the Apostolic Preaching,* trans. Joseph P. Smith (Westminster, MD: Newman Press, 1952), p. 51.

43   Robert Hugh Benson writes: 'Music, and its relation to man's inner nature, has not yet been adequately considered. All other arts are imitative or descriptive: music is creative. Painting imitates colours: not so music, a bird's song, or thunder. Music, it may well be, *rises from a spring within man himself,* and if imitative at all is *imitative of something beyond the world of sense*': quoted by C. C. Martindale in *The Life of Monsignor Robert Hugh Benson,* vol. 2 (London: Longmans, Green & Co., 1916), p. 344 (emphasis added).

44   *Freedom* here corresponds to Cassian's *purity of heart.* See John Cassian, *Conferences,* i.6–7, trans. Colm Luibheid (New York: Paulist Press, 1985), p. 39. By associating growth in inner freedom to the work of liturgical chant, the ascetical and aesthetical aspects of the liturgy, often seen in antinomy, are synthesised in the liturgy, the primary locus of personal and corporate conversion.

45   Zundel, *The Splendour of the Liturgy,* p. 78.

46   Clement of Alexandria, 'Protrepticus', quoted in James McKinnon (ed.), *Music in Early Christian Literature* (Cambridge University Press, 1987), p. 30.

47   This same theological anthropology is implicit in more recent liturgical law's defence of the irreplaceable value of human breath and human word in worship: 'The use of mechanical instruments and devices – such as the "player" organ, phonograph, radio, tape recorder or wire recorder, and other similar devices – is absolutely forbidden in liturgical services . . . even if their use is limited to transmitting sermons or sacred music, or substituting for the singing of the faithful or even supporting it': 'Instruction of the S. C. of Rites on Sacred Music and the Sacred Liturgy', 3 Sept. 1958, in Benedictine Monks (eds.), *The Liturgy, Papal Teachings* (Boston: St Paul Editions, 1962), pp. 603–04.

     The same position was reiterated after the Second Vatican Council: 'The Church wishes at all costs to maintain fidelity to that "worship in spirit and in truth" that the Lord Jesus has initiated. That brings in human beings, in their complete person, body and soul; their participation in the mystery of salvation, present sacramentally and at work, engages their whole being. Neither the celebrant, the people in the body of the church, nor the organist can be reduced to the status of a machine, a robot, a tape recorder. Theirs must be the presence of the holy people of God, praying, singing, playing music in a single-minded faith, a vital hope, and a burning charity': 'Mécanique et liturgie' (editorial) in *Notitiae* 3 (1967), pp. 3–4. See also Richard J. Schuler, 'Taped Music', *Sacred Music* 112 (1985), pp. 3–4.

48 The prohibition of musical instruments in favour of the unaccompanied human voice was universally observed in the West until the ninth century; in the East it is observed to this day. As late as 1749, Pope Benedict XIV was able to write: 'The use of the organ and musical instruments is not yet admitted by all the Christian world. . . . Our Pontifical Chapel, although allowing musical chant on condition that it be serious, decent and devout, has never allowed the organ. . . . No use is made of organ music; only vocal music, of grave rhythm, is allowed with plainchant': Benedict XIV, Encyclical *Annus Qui*, 19 Feb. 1749, in Benedictine Monks (eds.), *The Liturgy, Papal Teachings*, p. 53.

49 Cassiodorus, *Explanation of the Psalms*, vol. 1, trans. P. G. Walsh (New York: Paulist Press, 1990), p. 25.

50 Lossky, 'Some Thoughts on Liturgical Music', p. 8.

51 Evelyn Underhill, *Worship* (New York: Harper & Row, 1957), p. 21. Illustrating this, St John Cassian writes: 'Once when I was singing the psalms a verse of it put me in the way of the prayer of fire. Or sometimes the musical expression of a brother's voice has moved sluggish minds to the most intense prayer': *Conferences*, ix.26, trans. Luibheid, p. 117. The experiences described are not of the aesthetic order but rather illustrate the potential of liturgical chant to dispose the worshipper to a transforming encounter with the Holy.

52 Concerning the *Exultet*, R. H. Benson writes: 'It was a song such as none but a Christian could ever sing. It soared, dropped, quavered, leapt again, laughed, danced, rippled, sank, leapt once more, on and on, untiring and undismayed, like a stream running clear to the sea. Angels, earth, trumpets, Mother Church, all nations and all peoples sang in its singing. And I, in my stiff pew, smiled all over my face with sheer joy and love': quoted in Martindale, *The Life of Monsignor Robert Hugh Benson*, vol. 1, p. 293.

53 On recitation formulae for readings, see Hiley, *Western Plainchant*, pp. 154–58.

54 Examples from the Roman liturgy abound: the various dialogues and acclamations, the simple tone of the *Te Deum*, the brief responsories of Lauds and Vespers, Gloria XV, Credo I, and Sanctus XVIII.

55 'È la messa, Ordinario et Proprio, che si deve cantare, en non "qualcosa", anche se *plane congruit*, che si sovrappone alla Messa. Perché *l'azione* è unica, ha un solo volto, un solo accento, una sola voce: la voce della Chiesa. Continuare a cantare mottetti, sia pure devoti e pii (come il *Lauda Sion* all'offertorio nella festa di un santo), ma estranei alla Messa, *in luogo dei testi della Messa che si cerebra*, significa continuare un'ambiguità inammissibile: dare crusca invece di buon frumento, vinello annacquato invece di vino generoso. Perché non solo la melodia ce interessa nel canto liturgico, ma le parole, il testo, il pensiero, i sentimenti rivestiti di poesia et di melodia. Ora, questi testi devono essere quelli della

Messa, non altri. Cantare *la* Messa, dunque, e non solo cantare *durante* la Messa': 'Cantare la Messa et non cantare durante la Messa', *Notitiae* 5 (1969), p. 406.

56 The most comprehensive document of the post-conciliar period to treat of active sung participation in the liturgy is the instruction of the Sacred Congregation of Rites, *Musicam Sacram*, issued 5 March 1967 (see *Notitiae* 3 (1967), pp. 81–108). *Musicam Sacram* presents the sung celebration as normative. Of this normative form, the spoken celebration is an adaptation and accommodation. Contrary to a widely held misconception, the fully sung celebration is not a solemnisation of the spoken form of the liturgy; on the contrary, the spoken form is derived from the fully sung celebration, which is normative. See the (untitled) introduction to *Musicam Sacram* by L. Agustoni in *Notitiae* 3 (1967), p. 82.

57 Dumitru Staniloae, *Theology and the Church*, trans. Robert Barringer (Crestwood, NY: St Vladimir's Seminary Press, 1980), p. 71.

58 Rembert Herbert, 'Gregorian Chant in Context', *Monastic Studies* 19 (1991), p. 131.

59 The author's personal experience as a choirmaster is that it is far more difficult to teach people the worth of silence in the chant than to achieve a satisfactory vocal sound. What the chant leaves unsung is ultimately more important than what it sings. The quality of singing increases in proportion to the singer's awareness of the unsung mystery.

60 Herbert, 'Gregorian Chant in Context', p. 130.

61 Kavanagh, *On Liturgical Theology*, pp. 188–93.

62 'It is too obvious to be denied that a celebration sung in the Gregorian manner is more solemn than a celebration which is merely recited; but this statement is especially true in the modern perspective of a celebration which is habitually recited. The ancients had provided melodies for the most modest celebrations of the liturgical year, and these melodies were no less carefully worked out than those of the great feasts. For them the chant was, before all else, a means of giving to liturgical prayer a fullness of religious and contemplative value whatever might be the solemnity of the day. Such should also be our sole preoccupation in singing. As long as people look upon Gregorian chant solely as a means of solemnising the celebration, there will be the danger of making it deviate from its true path, which is more interior': Dominique Delalande, OP, 'Le Chant grégorien', in *Initiation théologique. Tome I: Les sources de la théologie* (Paris: Editions du Cerf, 1950), pp. 255–56.

Conclusion

The Spirit of the
Liturgical Movement

STRATFORD CALDECOTT

The chapters in this volume hardly reflect the full breadth of
the conference where they were originally delivered as papers,
and yet they capture the central theme. The theme is an
important one. It is located right at the point of intersection
between faith and culture. As a result, the response to the conference was both interesting and overwhelming. The Oxford
Declaration produced by a broad group of participants (see
Appendix) was both praised and scorned in the Catholic press
in the months that followed the conference. A flood of correspondence received by the Centre for Faith & Culture testified
to the enormous public interest in, and the intense emotions
aroused by, this subject. Catholic-minded Christians of all ages
and many backgrounds clearly felt outraged at the way the
liturgical tradition of the Catholic Church had been vandalised
in the period after the Second Vatican Coucil. Of course, they
differed in where they placed the blame, and what they
proposed the Church should now do to try to rectify the
situation. New groups and alignments within the Church must
now help to define the principles and procedures by which the
liturgical movement can contribute to the healing of the
Church, rather than its continued destruction.

Without a religious dimension, a culture has no heart, no
ultimate meaning. At one time, the liturgy of the Church
penetrated much of medieval Europe with continual reminders

of the presence of God. It also made possible a kind of harmony with nature, reflected in the great art, architecture and music of the Christian centuries.

It is arguable that all the arts of Christendom were 'born from the altar', i.e. developed in some way out of the act of worship, in the lap of Mary. The Church was a great patron, and the works she commissioned were very largely expressions of praise, praise for the supreme Artist, expressing himself in the creation and redemption of nature. But science too, it has been convincingly argued by historians from Pierre Duhem to Stanley Jaki, is a child of Christendom, a child of Mary. Scholastic philosophy, far from being an obstruction to intellectual progress, was the necessary precursor, the seedbed of scientific method.

As we all know, these children of Mary 'grew up', and before long had declared their independence, indeed claimed the right to vote. The developing natural sciences lost the sense that what they were investigating was something sacred, because made and sustained by the God 'in whom we live, and move, and have our being'. God himself was eventually disposed of as an 'unnecessary hypothesis', and the exploration of nature proceeded with less and less reference to the possibility that it might have an ultimate *meaning*. European culture became dominated by the metaphor of the Machine. The arts alternately reflected and reacted to this process.

A secular culture is one that views itself as adult, and tries to usurp the place of the divine Father, becoming Creator of its own artificial cosmos. It tends to identify knowledge with power. It values efficiency, speed, productivity and originality over empathy, human relationships, contemplation and tradition. It enthrones quantity over quality, masculine over feminine. (The Middle Ages had kept its balance by enshrining at its centre the image of the Madonna and Child.) Nature becomes a resource to be exploited, learned from and ultimately surpassed. All this we have seen in the history of Western civilisation, culminating in the Human Genome Project and the creation of the artificial dimension known as 'cyberspace'.

A human being cannot find peace of heart within such a culture. We are simply not made that way. Action that does not spring from contemplation, speech that does not arise from silence, a society that does not worship a reality higher than itself are not fully human. This being a fact of human nature we see, at the very climax of the rationalist culture, a breakdown of scientific materialism and the rediscovery of religion in a rich variety of forms. We experience two opposed tendencies. One leads towards a celebration of irrationalism and so to a kind of *nihilism* – not always a savage, despairing nihilism but more often a sophisticated, amusing, enticing decadence. (With social hierarchies overthrown, and the clear certainties of nineteenth-century science having dissolved into chaos or the ambiguities of wave–particle duality, meaning, order and morality have largely become a do-it-yourself affair. Many attempt to live without them, in an emptiness filled only by physical desire or psychological whim.) Opposed to this, another tendency leads – often via the New Age movement or the encounter with non-Christian religious traditions – in the direction of a recovery of the awareness of a transcendent reality and of an order at the heart of the universe. This process has been called the 're-enchantment of the world'.

Few in the rapidly-reviving liturgical movement want to reverse the last thirty years; most simply want to enrich the present mainstream reformed liturgy with more of a *sense of the sacred*. The encounter with other religions, and particularly with the mystical or contemplative dimension of other religions, may have helped to awaken them to this need, which began to find an official voice in the Extraordinary Synod of Bishops in 1985. Since then, Cardinal Joseph Ratzinger has become a major promoter of the idea of resacralisation. Catholic sociologists from Mary Douglas (*Natural Symbols*) to Kieran Flanagan (*Sociology and Liturgy*) have drawn our attention to the meaning of the sacred, and to the function of complex symbolism in public worship.

This new liturgical movement is characterised in part by calls for the restoration of elements of the Latin tradition that went out of fashion with liturgists after Vatican II: the 'body language' of posture and gesture, the use of incense, more elaborate and attractive vestments, and Gregorian chant – the latter reflected even in the popular music charts. An emphasis, perhaps an inevitable over-emphasis, on *under-standing the spoken word* accompanied the promulgation of the vernacular Mass during the 1960s and 1970s. But by now it has become clear that use of the vernacular alone is not enough to ensure the continuing 'active participation' of the laity. Indeed the Council's phrase *participatio actuosa* is coming to be understood less in terms of 'active participation' and more in terms of 'participation in the act'. Certainly the word 'active' (or better, 'dynamic') should not be taken as referring primarily to the physical behaviour of the congregation, but rather to its involvement in and through prayer – that is, to its interior (and to a large extent invisible) identification with the Church's act of worship.

Worship, however, must be a whole-body, a whole-person experience. This fuller participation can best be promoted not by the introduction of more physical activity (hymn-singing, liturgical dance, etc.) but by the greater use of the senses in liturgy, as well as a greater sensitivity to the richness of metaphor and controlled ambiguity in liturgical language. What we seem to be seeing, in general, is a growing awareness that *beauty* is a vital aspect of liturgical performance, conducive to 'active participation' in the deepest sense. The hope for a *rapproche-ment* with Eastern Orthodoxy, and the growing familiarity throughout the West with aspects of the rich Byzantine liturgical, theological and iconographic tradition (to a large extent already present within the Catholic Church through the Eastern rites), is another factor working in the same direction. The evident splendour and elaborate formality of the Oriental liturgies is not for all, but contact with it can still awaken an understanding of the original *purpose* of liturgy, and a longing for deep religious experience that may have been denied to those steeped in more action-oriented or secularised celebrations.

The danger to be avoided, of course, is that of falling back into a kind of mystification. But with the vernacular safely established and the laity thoroughly aroused I personally doubt this is a serious problem. An even greater danger now comes from presenting the Mass and the prayer life of the Church as something stale and prosaic, and therefore unrelated to the work of self-transformation. When this happens, and when the purpose of the sacraments comes to be seen in *moralistic* terms – as a way of inculcating good behaviour and loyalty to the Church of Rules – people vote with their feet, and flock to the New Age movement, where they will gladly fast, or spend days on their knees reciting mantras, or even learn Sanskrit, for a chance of experiencing a numinous reality beyond the ordinary. In such circumstances, the use of Latin or the re-introduction of traditional devotions to the Blessed Sacrament can help to revive the feeling that what is going on in the Mass is not a banal celebration of the community's solidarity with itself, but the sacred enactment of a ritual with truly cosmic significance – even if the inner meaning of the words and actions does not reveal itself without the accompaniment of silent prayer:

> What you have come to is nothing known to the senses: not a blazing fire, or a gloom turning to total darkness, or a storm; or trumpeting thunder or the great voice speaking which made everyone that heard it beg that no more should be said to them. . . . But what you have come to is Mount Zion and the city of the living God, the heavenly Jerusalem where the millions of angels have gathered for the festival, with the whole Church in which everyone is a 'first-born son' and a citizen of heaven. (Hebrews 12:18–19, 22–23)

The auguries are therefore good for a widespread revival of Catholic spirituality in the next century – perhaps reinvigorated by the expansion of the Church in the Third World, and the development of innumerable new movements and communities from Taizé to Focolare, from Neocatechumenate to the charismatics. Religious consciousness in general is mystical, poetic, sensitive to the many-layered meanings of symbolism, aware of the correspondences and analogies which bind the universe together. Catholicism and Orthodoxy provide a home for such a consciousness by being essentially *sacramental*. Even their ecclesial structures exist for the sake of the sacraments and the spiritual life these are designed to nourish. For this reason, any recovery of religious sensibility must in the long run work in favour of traditional sacramental and liturgical forms, even as it enriches and transforms them.

For a 'sacramental Christian', the life of Christ is distributed through the Church and throughout the liturgical year. We relive the entire cycle of his self-giving life, death, resurrection and sending of the Spirit. Time and space, drained of meaning by sin and secularism, can be resanctified by Christ's presence, flowing through the sacramental organism of his 'Mystical Body'. By participating in the Mass and the Church's daily prayer, baptised believers are caught up in Christ's sacrifice, so that all we are and do in our daily lives is given to the Father for him to raise from the dead. That fact is what energises, heals and transforms us in the common life of the Christian community.[1]

For Cardinal Joseph Ratzinger, the leading voice in the contemporary liturgical movement, 'Liturgy has a cosmic and universal dimension. The community does not become a community by mutual interaction. It receives its being as a gift from an already existing completeness, totality, and in return it gives itself back to this totality.' This is why, he adds, liturgy cannot be simply 'made'. It has to be *received* (from heaven or from tradition) and continually *revitalised*. Liturgy 'goes beyond the realm of what can be made and manipulated; it introduces us to the realm of given, living reality, which communicates itself to us. That is why, at all times and in all religions, the fundamental law of liturgy has been the law of organic growth within the universality of the common tradition.'[2]

The criticism by traditionalists of the liturgical reform initiated by the Second Vatican Council is in part due to the feeling that this *law of organic growth* was not sufficiently understood by the reformers of the late 1960s and early 1970s, and has been broken in actual fact by the way the liturgy was changed. Many of those changes were not foreseen by the Council Fathers, and it is arguable from the text of *Sacrosanctum Concilium* that they would not have approved of them. Nevertheless, they took place. We may take this as proving the limitations of the protection the Holy Spirit extends over the Church's decisions. That protection, it seems to me, is minimalistic, ensuring only the validity (*ex opere operato*) of the sacraments despite all the reformers can do to them. God wishes to allow the greatest scope for human freedom compatible with the universal offer of salvation through his Church. He must therefore preserve from error the Church's core teaching on faith and morals, and from destruction the sacraments through which the life of Christ is offered and extended through time and space.

The aesthetics of the liturgy are therefore vulnerable, and this is important because if the liturgical celebration is spoilt by the hands of men it will lose some of its power over the soul, its power to attract and to convert. It is all very well to be able to speak; but to *speak* is not the same as to communicate with those who do not already understand the message. Hans Urs von Balthasar makes a passionate plea for the importance of beauty at the opening of his *The Glory of the Lord*: 'No longer loved and fostered by religion, beauty is lifted from its face as a mask, and its absence exposes features on that face which threaten to become incomprehensible to man.' He adds, 'We can be sure that whoever sneers at her name as if she were the ornament of a bourgeois past – whether he admits it or not – can no longer pray and soon will no longer be able to love.' In a world that has tried to dispense with beauty, 'Man stands before the good and asks himself why *it* must be done and not rather its alternative, evil. Or this, too, is a possibility, and even the more exciting one: Why not investigate Satan's depths?' Beauty is the 'neglected sister' of Truth and Goodness, the three transcendental properties of Being. Without her, we lose them too. We may still be able to speak the truth in syllogisms, like an infallible computer, but 'the logic of these answers is itself a mechanism which no longer captivates anyone'.[3]

Yet at the same time, von Balthasar draws an important distinction between 'beauty' and divine 'glory' (*kabod, doxa, gloria*), between an 'aesthetic theology' and a 'theological aesthetics'. As we have seen and know only too well, the divine liturgy in the hands of men is not always beautiful, not always charming or enticing. It does not always raise the heart and mind towards God on flights of music or floods of emotion. It may cast us down, from time to time, in despair or depression. It may function more to distract than to focus our prayer. Yet despite that, it is always – by virtue of God's action, not our own

– the expression of the supreme beauty, the splendour, of the self-giving of the Father and the Son. So von Balthasar is able to say that the 'polished, aesthetic dignity' of the form must not be allowed to predominate over the 'perennially new, non-objectifiable dignity of the divine event' with which the Mass is to be ultimately identified. 'The awareness of inherent glory gave inspiration to works of incomparable earthly beauty in the great tradition of the Church. But these works become suitable for today's liturgy only if, in and beyond their beauty, those who take part are not merely moved to aesthetic sentiments but are able to encounter that glory of God to which the Creator wanted to lead such works.'[4]

Romano Guardini, in his little book *The Spirit of the Liturgy*, speaks of art as an attempt to overcome discord, to reconcile the contradiction between what we are and what we wish to be. But, he goes on, 'The liturgy offers something higher. In it man, with the aid of grace, is given the opportunity of realizing his fundamental essence, of really becoming that which according to his divine destiny he should be and longs to be, a child of God.' And so the liturgy adopts suitable forms and methods from the sphere of art. 'It speaks measuredly and melodiously; it employs formal, rhythmic gestures; it is clothed in colours and garments foreign to everyday life; it is carried out in places and at hours which have been co-ordinated and systematised according to sublimer laws than ours. It is in the highest sense the life of a child, in which everything is picture, melody and song.'[5]

Children, as any parent will testify, are naturally liturgical creatures. They love rituals and do their best to invent them at every opportunity. The spirit of the liturgy is the spirit of a child. As Guardini says, the liturgy 'unites art and reality in a supernatural childhood before God'. It is a way of *being at play* – like the angels, 'who, without a purpose and as the Spirit stirs them, move before God, and are a mystic diversion and a living song before him'; or like the eternal Wisdom, who 'was with him, forming all things, and was delighted every day, playing before him at all times, playing in the world' (Proverbs 8:30–31). That explains the repetition, the formalism, the dressing up, and above all the 'sublime mingling of profound earnestness and divine joyfulness' that we find in the Mass. It is, of course, nothing but a complete *waste of time* if we regard ourselves as too grown up and too busy to play at being God's kingdom.

The true spirit of the liturgy is most clearly revealed when the Mass or the Divine Office is chanted or sung, rather than simply said. The transformation of the words of the liturgy *into music* allows them to resonate throughout the soul and to engage our feelings as well as our thoughts. It also helps us enter more fully into a different sense of time, indeed into the timelessness (aeviternity) of the kingdom of God. When the spirit of this-worldliness entered into and distorted the reform of the liturgy, one of the first things that came under attack was the tradition of sacred music and liturgical chant. This was a direct assault not only on the beauty but on the playfulness of the liturgy, which depends on a sense of being 'with the angels'. 'See that you do not despise one of these little ones; for I tell you that in heaven their angels always behold the face of my Father who is in heaven' (Matthew 18:10).

In the same passage of the Gospel, Jesus tells his disciples: 'Unless you turn and become like children, you will never enter the kingdom of heaven' (Matthew 18:3). In a collection of essays entitled *Journey towards Easter*, Joseph Ratzinger explores the 'theological significance of the infancy of Jesus', and of the 'eminence' that Jesus himself conferred on being a child. For the Son of God, the essence of his existence and his mission is to be the child of the eternal Father, to be dependent upon him, to be turned towards him, to love him, and so to represent him. Even his last, despairing cry from the Cross was addressed to the Father. Childhood in this sense of dependence, of being free of all possessions, of receiving everything from another, is not something we leave behind us when we grow to biological adulthood. It is the state into which we must grow, consciously – becoming (as we are told by Ste Thérèse) littler and littler, until we enter again the womb of the Mother, and are reborn as 'other Christs', sons in the Son.[6]

Ratzinger, Guardini and Balthasar are almost one voice in this, as they expose the deepest principles of the liturgical movement. To understand and be faithful to the spirit of the liturgical movement which they represent we must understand 'supernatural childhood'. Without that spirit, any reform of the liturgy will resemble the clumsy interference of a grown-up in the game of a divine Child. If I found my daughters playing shops, and insisted that they use real money and account for every penny, making a profit at the end of the day or go out of business, they would quickly lose interest and walk away. If I find the Holy Trinity playing 'school of prayer', I should be wary of insisting, just because I am an expert at real life, on changing the rules to make it all more didactic, more entertaining, more comforting – in a word, more 'efficient'.

To be a child is to be turned not only to the Father, but to be turned first to the Mother, and it is from the Mother that we learn what it is to be a child – the Mother, for whom the Father and the Child are within. The Mother conceives by listening, and after she has conceived 'ponders all these things in her heart'. Divine liturgy is the pondering, the treasuring of memories, the contemplation ever repeated as though for the first time of the love of the Father, and the repetition of the *fiat* in which the Child is conceived, on earth as it is in heaven. In the liturgy we learn to listen, to wait, to ripen. We must become silent in order to welcome the silent Word. As Maurice Zundel writes in *Our Lady of Wisdom*, 'She offers her transparence as a pure window to the sun, and the Mystery of Jesus flames through her unhindered.'[7] At that depth of life, all the 'events of the past find in Christ their meaning and fullness, and creation is revealed for what it is: a complex whole which finds its perfection, its purpose *in the liturgy* alone'.[8]

Notes

1   This paragraph grows out of private correspondence with Miss Meriol Trevor.

2   J. Ratzinger, *The Feast of Faith* (San Francisco, CA: Ignatius Press, 1986), p. 66.

3   H. U. von Balthasar, *The Glory of the Lord: A Theological Aesthetics*, I, *Seeing the Form* (Edinburgh and San Francisco, CA: T&T Clark and Ignatius Press, 1982), pp. 18–19.

4 H. U. von Balthasar, *New Elucidations* (San Francisco, CA: Ignatius Press, 1986), p. 136.

5 R. Guardini, *The Church and the Catholic, and The Spirit of the Liturgy* (London: Sheed & Ward, 1935), pp. 180–81. See also the same author's *Meditations before Mass* (Manchester, NH: Sophia Institute Press, 1993).

6 J. Ratzinger, *Journey towards Easter* (New York: Crossroad, 1987), pp. 70–74.

7 M. Zundel, *Our Lady of Wisdom* (New York: Sheed & Ward, 1940), p. 38.

8 John Paul II, *Orientale Lumen* (1995).

List of Contributors

CHRISTOPHER ZEALLEY is a bookseller specialising in Catholic books, currently writing a D.Phil thesis at Wolfson College, Oxford, on Christian spirituality in eighteenth-century Britain.

M. FRANCIS MANNION is Rector of the Cathedral of the Madeleine and Theological Advisor in the Diocese of Salt Lake City, Utah. He is President of the Society for Catholic Liturgy, formed in 1995.

MARK DREW trained for the priesthood in Oxford, Germany and France, and was ordained in the Diocese of Sens, in one of the most dechristianised parts of France, where he is in charge of a country parish.

SERGE KELEHER studied Liturgy under Alexander Schmemann, Louis Bouyer and Boniface Luykx. A Greek-Catholic Archimandrite, he edits *Eastern Churches Journal*, and lives in Dublin, Ireland.

EAMON DUFFY is Reader in Church History in the University of Cambridge, and a Fellow of Magdalene College. He is the author of the well-known study of the English Reformation, *The Stripping of the Altars*, and is a Board member of the Society for Catholic Liturgy.

MARC-DANIEL KIRBY, O.Cist., teaches Liturgics and Spirituality at Holy Apostles Seminary in Cromwell, Connecticut.

STRATFORD CALDECOTT is the Director and founder of the Centre for Faith & Culture, and a Research Fellow in the Department of Theology at Westminster College, Oxford.

Appendix

The Oxford Declaration on Liturgy

Issued by the Liturgy Forum of the Centre for Faith & Culture at Westminster College, Oxford, at the conclusion of the 1996 Conference of the Centre, 'Beyond the Prosaic'

1. Reflecting on the history of liturgical renewal and reform since the Second Vatican Council, the Liturgy Forum agreed that there have been many positive results. Among these might be mentioned the introduction of the vernacular, the opening up of the treasury of the Sacred Scriptures, increased participation in the liturgy and the enrichment of the process of Christian initiation. However, the Forum concluded that the pre-conciliar liturgical movement as well as the manifest intentions of *Sacrosanctum Concilium* have in large part been frustrated by powerful contrary forces, which could be described as bureaucratic, philistine and secularist.

2. The effect has been to deprive the Catholic people of much of their liturgical heritage. Certainly, many ancient traditions of sacred music, art and architecture have been all but destroyed. *Sacrosanctum Concilium* gave pride of place to Gregorian chant (Article 116), yet in many places this 'sung theology' of the Roman liturgy has disappeared without trace. Our liturgical heritage is not a superficial embellishment of worship but should properly be regarded as intrinsic to it, as it is also to the process of transmitting the Catholic faith in education and evangelisation. Liturgy cannot be separated from culture; it is the living font of a Christian civilisation and hence has profound ecumenical significance.

3. The impoverishment of our liturgy after the Council is a fact not yet sufficiently admitted or understood, to which the necessary response must be a *revival of the liturgical movement* and the initiation of a new cycle of reflection and reform. The liturgical movement which we represent is concerned with the enrichment, correction and resacralisation of Catholic liturgical practice. It is concerned with a renewal of liturgical eschatology, cosmology and aesthetics, and with a recovery of the sense of the sacred – mindful that the law of worship is the law of belief. This renewal will be aided by a closer and deeper acquaintance with the liturgical, theological and iconographic traditions of the *Christian East.*

4. The revived liturgical movement calls for the promotion of the *Liturgy of the Hours,* celebrated in song as an action of the Church in cathedrals, parishes, monasteries and families, and of *Eucharistic Adoration,* already spreading in many parishes. In this way, the Divine Word and the Presence of Christ's reality in the Mass may resonate throughout the day, making human culture into a dwelling-place for God. At the heart of the Church in the world we must be able to find that loving contemplation, that adoring silence, which is the essential complement to the spoken word of Revelation, and the key to active participation in the holy mysteries of faith.[1]

5. We call for a greater *pluralism* of Catholic rites and uses, so that all these elements of our tradition may flourish and be more widely known during the period of reflection and *ressourcement* that lies ahead. If the liturgical movement is to prosper, it must seek to rise above differences of opinion and taste to that unity which is the Holy Spirit's gift to the Body of Christ. Those who love the Catholic tradition in its fullness should strive to *work together in charity,* bearing each other's burdens in the light of the Holy Spirit, and persevering in prayer with Mary the Mother of Jesus.

6. We hope that any future liturgical reform would not be imposed on the faithful but would proceed, with the utmost caution and sensitivity to the *sensus fidelium,* from a thorough

understanding of the organic nature of the liturgical traditions of the Church.[2] Our work should be sustained by prayer, education and study. This cannot be undertaken in haste, or in anything other than a serene spirit. No matter what difficulties lie ahead, the glory of the Paschal Mystery – Christ's love, his cosmic sacrifice and his childlike trust in the Father – shines through every Catholic liturgy for those who have eyes to see, and in this undeserved grace we await the return of spring.

29 June 1996
St Peter and St Paul

Notes

1   Cf. *Orientale Lumen*, Article 16.
2   Cf. *Sacrosanctum Concilium*, Article 23.

Index of Names

Adam, Karl 42 n55
Adoremus: The Society for the
   Renewal of the Sacred Liturgy
   3, 4, 7, 19, 20, 21, 40 n40
Aerath, Chacko 42 n56
Agustoni, L. 148 n56
Angelica, Mother 3
Aquinas, Saint Thomas 26
Archer, Anthony 48 n84
Association for Latin Liturgy 39
   n29
Augustine, Saint 63, 119, 120

Bacci, Antonio 38 n15, 52
Baker, Kenneth 3
Balasuriya, Tissa 41 n46
Balthasar, Hans Urs von 31, 46
   n76, 155–56, 157–58, 158 n3,
   159 n4
Barth, Karl 51
Basil, Saint 86, 128
Baumstark, Anton 70
Beall, Stephen M. 41 n41
Beauduin, Lambert 70, 73, 74, 88,
   90 n7, 91 n15, 141
Beeck, Frans Josef van 43 n61
Beinert, Wolfgang 42 n55
Benedict XIV, Pope 147 n48
Benson, Robert Hugh 146 n43, 147
   n52

Berger, Peter 47 n79
Bergh, Thomas 71
Berry, Mary 91 n14
Bishop, Edmund 97–98, 101, 106,
   125 n1
Borello, Andrew 40 n41
Botte, Bernard 70
Bouyer, Louis 43 n61, 45 n69,
   30–31, 51, 70, 73–74, 75, 76–77,
   90 n9, 91 nn10, 11, 16, 18, 94
   n58
Bradshaw, Paul 46 n74
Brown, Frank Burch 44 n64
Brown, Raymond E. 17
Bugnini, Annibale 13, 37 n6,
   54–55, 83, 94 n65
Burghardt, Walter J. 41 n43

Carminati, Giancarlo 145 n35
Casel, Odo 70, 74
Cassian, Saint John 146 n44, 147
   n51
Cassiodorus, Flavius Magnus
   Aurelius 147 n49
Centre for Faith & Culture 2, 4,
   149
Chupungco, Anscar J. 23
CIEL, see International Centre for
   Liturgical Studies
Cippola, Richard G. 44 n65